# EDIT YOUR OWN ROMANCE NOVEL

## 3-BOOKS IN 1. BACKBURNING BACKSTORY, THE 13 MAIN SCENES AND THE STAIRCASE OF TURNING POINTS

EBONY MCKENNA

EBONY MCKENNA

Edit Your Own Romance Novel

© Ebony McKenna 2017

Paperback edition © 2018

ISBN 978-0-9953839-8-2

# CONTENTS

# INTRODUCTION

Hi there, I'm Ebony McKenna, I'm an Australian author of seven published young adult romances, a handful of short stories, three non–fiction writing guides and dozens of ideas and half–written *things* in the bottom drawer. I also write science fiction as E.J. McKenna.

This *Edit Your Own Romance Novel* book will help you become objective about your own work and help you get rid of all the things that weigh a story down.

I'll show you how to get out of your own way and let the reader get on with enjoying the story.

Quick note: As I said earlier, I'm Australian, so this editing book is full of what some regard as spelling mistakes. They're not. I'm using Australian spelling throughout, so you'll see the 'u' sneak into words like 'colour' and 'flavour' and your usual 'ize' will soften to 'ise' but still sound the same. This is all perfectly OK. The important thing to remember with spelling is to be consistent. Choose your favourite kind of spelling and stick with it.

I repeat myself, and often, because deep down, I know you're going to ignore me the first time I suggest doing something that you don't particularly feel like doing.

Because you will sort of think it doesn't really apply to you and so you don't really need to do it, right? But after a while, sometimes after many whiles, you'll realise it *does* apply to you and you will do it.

There may be times over the next few weeks where you think, "oh that's ok, you're just repeating yourself like you said you would, that doesn't apply to me."

It does.

"But Ebony–"

No, really, it does. And yes, I'm repeating myself, because it's important.

BEFORE WE EVEN START (how annoying is this? You're so ready to go and I'm holding you back. This is what backstory does to your novel, ps.) The very first editing step you need to take comes immediately after typing 'The end' on a draft.

That step is this:

- Put your manuscript in the 'bottom drawer'.
- Don't even look at it for at least a month.
- Three months is even better.
- Start your next project so you become completely distracted with your new shiny thing.

OK, that was four steps, but you get my drift.

"But Ebony!" I hear you scream. "I'm here to learn about editing workshop. You can't blow us off like that!"

This is perfectly true. I'm not phoning it in. But the best way to be objective about your own work is to read a manuscript you haven't immediately finished working on. You'll come back to it with fresh eyes and fresh ideas.

If this isn't possible, please don't stress. Do your best, knowing that the skills you learn in this workshop will work for your current project and later projects. If at all possible, get in the habit of 'leap–frogging' projects – leaving one and going back to an earlier one, then when that's done, grab the one from before. If that works for you.

If it doesn't then that's fine too.

Caveat: Every book (especially mine) will always benefit from a completely new set of eyes going over it. By using this book as a guide, your manuscript will be in better shape and be a better book for it. That means you'll spend less money hiring an editor if you're self–publishing (because time is money and it's better to waste your own time first instead of wasting money). If going the traditional route, you'll have a better–quality manuscript for publishers and agents when you're submitting.

OK, are you ready to become your own editor?

Cool!

# PART I

BACKBURNING BACKSTORY - OTHERWISE
KNOWN AS THE AUTHOR GETTING OUT OF
THEIR OWN WAY.

# THE PROPER RULES OF ROMANCE

So many people have strange ideas that romance novels are written to a strict formula (which is both true and a load of rubbish at the same time) and that things have to happen on set pages. Forget everything you've heard ill-informed people say about 'the romance writing formula'. Those old (seriously old) zombie–rumours that refuse to die. You know the ones I'm talking about:

'You just write to Harlequin and they send you the formula, first kiss on page 16, first shag on page 148.'

'All romance novels are the same.'

'You just fill in the blanks.'

'Happy endings are so unbelievable and such an easy cop–out.' This last one drives me bonkers, because a proper, satisfying happy ending is really, really hard to get just right.

People who disparage romance and any kind of structure or formula do my head in, because what they're really saying is, 'it's far easier for me to scorn something I don't understand than to embrace it and perhaps even enjoy it.'

Don't be scared of structure, formula or formats because when you are guided by structure, formula and format, you are actually delivering on the goods for your reader. My job is to help you fall in love with structure. More specifically, a romance–novel–friendly structure involving 13 major scenes that your romance novel needs to have in order to satisfy your readers.

Because writing isn't actually about you. It's about your readers. You are doing something for them; you are entertaining them. And readers are fussy creatures who want a novel to be 'just right' or they'll move on to the next one written by someone else.

We'll embrace structure and formula using scene cards, so get yourself a stack from your local newsagent/stationer and some colour markers, because sometimes you have to pretty things up to get things done.

Before we embrace formula, I'm putting this out there right now: There's a huge difference between formula and formulaic!

Formula gives us amazing, creative and entertaining movies like *Wonder Woman*, *Romancing The Stone* and *Bridesmaids*.

Formulaic gives us . . . basically everything below 20% on Rotten Tomatoes.

One hard and fast rule of romance novels – because it is the very definition of a romance novel – is that the story must have a happy ending.

If your story doesn't have a happy ending, then it's quite possibly lovely fiction, but you cannot 'brand' it as a romance novel, nor can you market it to romance readers as a 'romance novel'. You won't be giving them a 'surprise' or a 'twist on the genre', you'll be mightily pissing them off.

Romance readers want that happy ending. The happy ending is the entire reason people read romance. The readers are expecting it, and they want something expected yet unexpected and a bit of a twist but not crazy twist and predictable yet surprising.

Got that?

Because we're not in it to find out *if* they get together (and I count myself as a romance reader of long standing). We're in it to find out *how* they get together.

If romance readers want to read something different (which we very often do because we are voracious readers) then they will find that in general fiction, genre fiction, science fiction etc.

Respect the genre you're writing in. The happy ending is not a 'cop out'. It's actually very difficult to achieve because it needs to be satisfying, somewhat expected but also completely delightful. It needs to be a logical yet surprising conclusion to satisfy the reader. Above all it must be happy.

**Happy can be defined three ways:**

Happily Ever After – the couple are utterly committed to each other to the exclusion of all others, for the rest of their lives. Whether they get married or simply know they are soul mates and nothing will ever break them apart again, they will always be together.

Hopefully Ever After – often used in multi–book story arcs, where the couple are together at the end of one book, but the audience (and the characters) know they have further adventures and disasters awaiting them. They will stick together and see it through. The end tone is up–beat and there is a strong hope that the two main characters will end up together eventually (kind of like the ending to Gone With The Wind).

Happy For Now – an upbeat ending where both protagonists are in love and committed to each other, but for logical reasons (perhaps they're teenagers and they have long lives ahead of them and who knows what life will throw at them?) there isn't an expectation that they will always be together forever. Happy For Now is on the teetering edge of what is acceptable in a romance novel, because it's no guarantee they really will be committed to each other for the rest of their lives.

~

There are many sub–rules that follow on from the Happy Ever After Rule. They are THE THINGS THAT ARE NOT ALLOWED TO HAPPEN IN A ROMANCE NOVEL BECAUSE IF THEY DO IT'S NOT A ROMANCE NOVEL, it's just a novel:

1. A hero or heroine who dies. Yes, your favourite movie of all time, *Ghost*, is not 'a romance'. It's very *romantic* and wonderful at times, and there is good emotional closure at the end, but – spoilers – he's dead. If she had died and they met up together as ghosts at the end of the movie, then that would be different.

2. The relationship is not between true equals. This is a tricky one, because many romances are centred around people whom society decides are not equal. For example, a Duke and a scullery maid. At first, they're obviously not equals in social class – but events throughout the book will prove they are true equals in the emotional sense, and they are both happy at the end because they are a really good match for each other.

3. One of them has a crippling drug/gambling/vice habit. The addiction will always come first, and the relationship will be a distant second. This will not deliver a happy ending.

4. One of them is an elite athlete. Sports stars don't often make great romance leads because the game (and the club) will always take precedence over everything else in their lives. If, however, the hero/heroine is a coach or

former elite athlete, then the relationship can take centre stage and flourish. Yes, there are examples of writers who have broken this rule, and there's a whole line of romance novels tied in with car racing, football, winter sports etc, but generally speaking elite athletes don't really work that well in romance.

5. The power is unbalanced. (which is a tangent of the relationship not being between true equals) If you have a relationship between a slave and his or her owner (whether a historical slave, contemporary slave or outer space scifi slave) then the slave didn't really have a choice in the matter, did she? (or he?) If this is how the story starts, a lot of things have to happen in the plot and character development in order for the couple to have a balance of power. Oh, hi there Stockholm Syndrome! Which leads me to my next point, and it's an absolute doozy.

6. A lack of consent. Super important. Both parties need to be willing to come to the party (oooer!) If one of them isn't, or they're badgered into it until they eventually give in, then it's not a romance.

7. One or both of them is still married. Just no. If they're already married, then what's keeping them apart is their duty to another person – which is an *external* conflict. Excellent romance novels focus on the *internal* conflict, their internal beliefs that keep them from finding happiness. *Lady Chatterly's Lover* was not 'a romance' however deeply romantic it was in places. But hello, she was married.

YOU STILL HAVEN'T SAID WHAT PAGE THEY SHOULD HAVE THEIR FIRST KISS!

I haven't, because there is no rule for what page the first kiss should be on. Because it all depends on what kind of book you're writing. The romancebooks I write are young adult romances that have a sweet tone. I want to build to that first kiss so that it acts as a payoff for the reader and creates an emotional turning point for the characters. But kissing is pretty much as far as it goes in my books. Other writers and audiences will require a *lot* more.

There are guidelines if you're writing for a specific line with a publisher like Harlequin. For example, Medical romances will take place in a medical setting, that's a rule for that line, but they can be super sweet or hot enough to melt your slippers.

Sweet romances have kissing and lots of tension, but no really overt raunchy–raunch. If the couple gets together in the bedroom, it's hinted at rather than written on the page. They call it 'closing the bedroom door'.

Clean reads are becoming popular. Anything that could get a G or at the most a PG rating if it were made into a movie, would qualify as 'clean' in some circles. (I'm talking contemporary PG, not '80s PG' as we call it in our house, where we show a classic movie to our son and find it's not as 'mild' as we remember.) There are some clean reads that have no more than hand holding. This is fine, it's still a romance because the couple resolve their internal conflicts in a satisfying way and get a happy ending.

There are many other genres within the romance umbrella, right through to blazing hot reads that leave absolutely nothing to the imagination. They can also have three or more parties to the heat, and some of them can be shape shifting were panthers. Whatever floats your goat – if the couple (or trio or quad) are all willing, and they're all committed and happy at the end, it's a romance.

~

Here are more rules for your novel to be considered a 'romance' and satisfy the voracious romance reader:

- The central characters who are to fall in love, need to meet pretty early on in the story. It's absolutely fine if it's bleedingly obvious they will get together in the end. A romance novel is not based on 'will they or won't they?' That's not what the readers are in it for. The readers want to know how they get together (yes I'm repeating myself because it's important). They want to see how the characters sort themselves out, resolve those crippling internal conflicts and make it work.

- The main characters need to bring pre–existing personal conflicts to the story, which prevents them from getting together right away. This emotional baggage needs to be deep–seated and essential to who they are as a person. This is the engine that keeps all good romance novels motoring along. They must be deep–seated beliefs, not merely a misunderstanding. If they're both hot for each other from the beginning, it's their internal conflicts that hold them back.

- Once they start to feel the feelings for each other, they need to stop seeing other people. The journey to falling in love and making a lasting commitment to each other must be central to the story. If she's still hooking up with exes or he's still playing the field . . . it's not really a romance. It's a story with romance in it, but it's not 'a romance' which fulfils all the above criteria.

- There needs to be a threat to their happiness (the black moment), and it needs to be the result of the personal baggage they brought with them. It needs to be something that is their own doing, their own fault. They

9

then need to fight for their happiness, because true love
is worth fighting for.

- They need to shag on page 148.
- Just kidding, it's really pages 63, 91 and 152.

There are always examples where authors have broken these
rules. The reason they get away with it is because they're incredibly
talented and their writing is gorgeous.

# BACKBURNING BACKSTORY

*E*very competition entry I've read in the past year (and in the years before that) has started strongly. (Huge congrats if you've entered a romance writing competition in Australia, I may have been your judge!) Alas, many entries became tangled in backstory before the actual story could get started. A few pages in to a new story, I'm getting to know the characters and BAM! Flash back to four months ago. Of four years. Or more.

The reason I've brought Backburning Backstory to the front of this book is because it needs to be dealt with before anything else.

Writing backstory is an easy trap for a writer to fall into. From an editing point of view, it's also an easy problem to spot and fix. Once you use these visual techniques, you'll see the backstory for yourself and you'll be on your way to fixing it. This will give you early success (I'm all about results!) and motivate you to stick with the program.

Why should you remove backstory?

Because it runs the risk of becoming an infodump of 'tell' and good writing is all about showing not telling, and it's all about inviting readers in to your world.

Let me wrap myself in backstory. I'm perfectly happy here.

Backstory makes a reader sit in the corner and wait while the author writes themselves into a cosy spot about the history of her characters. And, if I may repeat myself, it's not about the author being comfortable, it's about the reader having a good time.

Let's light some fires and get ready to burn some backstory!
Step 1:

- Open your file – make sure it's the most recently saved version and you don't accidentally open an earlier draft.
- Now rename it so you know which file you're working on from here.

- Save your work regularly. I say this for my own benefit as well as yours!

Step2:

- Print out the first few chapters and get ready with any colour highlighter you like.

If you don't have a printer or you want to save paper, open the file and activate the highlighter in the formatting section. If you can't find it, type 'where is the highlight function on a XYZ Model 99 computer' into a search engine and the internet will give it to you.

---

Please also put the zoom function up to 150 or 175 % so the font is larger on your screen. This will help you spot annoying tpyos.

---

Step3:

- **Read your story out loud**. I can't stress this enough, so I've put it in bold. Reading out loud slows you down and helps you hear the rhythm of the story more clearly.
- Highlight text every time the character / narrator goes into memory, or thinks about something that happened before the story began – anything from childhood, anything the previous week, month, year etc.
- Highlight 'exposition' and explanations. Exposition is 'tell' and for the first few chapters you don't want to slow your reader down by 'telling' them anything. Your

book is about showing your reader a good time. Give it
to them.

- Any colour will do, as long as it stands out and you can
see it on the page.
- You can even mix and match if you want. Blue for his
backstory and pink for hers, if you need to differentiate.

Highlighting on the page is a technique the fabulous Margie
Lawson uses to great effect in her editing workshops. I was lucky
enough to attend her Friday workshop at the 2015 RWAustralia
conference in Melbourne. Highlighting various aspects of the
manuscript immediately helped me 'see' what was working and
what was not. She didn't cover 'backstory' per se, but she did make
us highlight 'thoughts' in yellow. This is my way of saying, 'I'm
inspired by Margie, but I'm not ripping her off.'

Here's what the first two pages of your manuscript might look
like when you highlight the backstory. This is something fun I'm
playing with – Pride and Prejudice and Bogans.

Don't worry that you can't read the text itself, this is just to
show you how much backstory found its way into the opening two
pages of my first draft.

*Chapter One*
*The 'meet cute', in which our hero and heroine meet, and it's not cute.*

IT is a truth universally acknowledged, that privileged young man in possession of a good fortune needs taking down a peg or three.

You could tell by the expensive European cars pulling up to the rusty school fence that the posh snobs were here. Times like this, Liz Bennet, future valedictorian of Magnolia Heights Secondary College, wished she'd been more sporty. Her sister, Jayney, had all the luck. Strong legs, strong lungs, and a strong kick to the shins that she always made look like an accident.
At least Jayney could get her aggro out on the soccer field. Liz had no such access to casual violence. She had to keep cool and beat these snobs by talking them into submission. That's how you won a debate.
She worried the inside of her cheek as she sized up the students from Fairborn College. The boys wore navy blue blazers and the girls wore something closer to a royal blue. They walked as if they were born with silver spoons up their arses. Just one of the Fairborn blazers probably cost more than Liz's entire summer and winter uniforms put together.
Which was a good thing. These indulged, expensive children would underestimate their opponents.
Magnolia Heights wasn't even supposed to have made it this far in the inter-school debating competition. In fact,

Liz and her team had done such a good job in their league, they'd been accepted - grudgingly - into the posh squads.
And here they were now, in the semi final for the entire western Victorian district. If they beat Fairborn, they'd get a weekend in Melbourne to take on the winners of the some other district and become sectional champions! Or whatever it was called.
The tallest of the lot strolled in to view, his hand extended towards Liz. "FitzWilliam Darcy. Would you kindly show us to the debating halls. Plus the change rooms for our football team."
Halls plural? Yeah, his school probably had a hall to get to all the other halls.
And also, what kind of pompous geezer called their child Fitzwilliam? Lol.
Pasting on a smile, she returned with, "I'm Liz, captain of the Steelers." That was the name of their debating team. "Welcome to Magnolia Heights. Thanks for coming so far out of your way. I'm heading to the hall now, and the girls toilet block is just down that path."
Fitzwilliam - seriously, what a gack-worthy name - turned to one of the girls behind him and said, "Good luck Charlie."
"Come on ladies," the one called Charlie said as she directed her players down the path.
"It's not an actual toilet block, is it?" One of them said loudly enough for Liz to hear.
"We're here by invitation, we're representing the school," Charlie shot back.

Grey highlighter on black and white text doesn't look quite as pretty as I'd hoped. But it gives the general idea.

Would you look at all that backstory! Straight away, I can see what needs cutting. It might have felt important to me as I'd begun writing the story, but I can see now that it's not needed in the finished product. Readers are smart. Those first two sentences show the reader all they need to know. They don't need to be told Liz will be a future valedictorian. We'll see that in everything she says and does.

Also, the story starts with Liz then immediately goes to Jayney – at a time in the text where we've barely met Liz. We need more of Liz, we need to see things through her eyes. We need to get to know her through her actions and dialogue, before chopping and changing the point of view to other people.

When I edit this, I will delete the highlighted/ darker shaded sections. All of it!

Do you have huge slabs of highlighted text? Do yourself a favour right now and delete all of it.

"But then I won't have a 50,000–word novel any more, I'll lose the first two chapters and have to write more!"

If this is the case, copy and paste your highlighted backstory into a new file called 'Novel off–cuts'. I do this with just about every manuscript, because I always find scenes that don't add anything to the story. Pasting the text into a holding file means you never lose that writing. It won't be wasted. Sure, your word count will drop – but this is the point of editing. You need to cut out the stuff that doesn't work early on. Later on, you will see where you can put in new scenes that help the story, so your word count will go back up – and they'll be usable words.

Uh oh, you're about to cry?

It's OK, I cry too at this point.

Sheer frustration because I didn't get it right the first time. But honestly, who does? You've written the backstory in the first place so that you, the writer, can get inside your characters' heads. But now you need to slash the backstory because your reader will want to get into the story as quickly as possible. Your reader (who is really smart) doesn't want to know everything about the characters all at once. They want to get to know the characters through their actions and dialogue as it plays out – on the page – not as 'I remember when' or 'this is why we're all here' moments.

Imagine you're at a party, and you meet a new person. You want small talk at first, because you've just met them. You don't want their entire life story / tale of woe / history of medical ailments because you've only just met them. It's the same with books.

## THE PSYCHOLOGY OF WRITING:

How and why does Backstory sneak in?

Many writers (myself included) write backstory subconsciously as a way of writing their way into the story. This is fine in the draft stage, but it needs to go. Why? Because you're getting in the way of your own story. Have confidence that the story can show readers what's going on, rather than you having to step in and tell people what the story is about.

Keep highlighting backstory and you will see how much you can cut from your first few chapters.

Why the first few chapters? Instinct tells me most of your backstory will be in the first three chapters. After that, you'll have written yourself into the story, the plot and characters will be in full flow and you won't feel the need to keep interrupting yourself with slabs of memories or 'how did we get here's'.

Keep going through the entire manuscript. You may find you're about to cut 10,000 words. Maybe more. Excellent! (Please stop crying. OK, fine, have a tissue.) That's 10,000 words of 'hold on a minute I have to tell the reader something that will delay them from enjoying the story'. That's 10,000 words of theoretical throat clearing and 'now see here, come sit down and I'll tell you thing or two'.

The story will rocket along now, unburdened. Your characters will come alive on the page, revealing their true selves to the reader, with their words and actions, in real time.

Write without fear
Edit without mercy

## BUT WHAT IF MY BACKSTORY IS REALLY IMPORTANT?

I'm so glad you asked. I know you're not asking just because you think deleting backstory doesn't apply to you.

It applies to everyone.

Backstory is important if a past trauma or character–building incident has played a major part in creating your character's belief system and inner conflicts. You need to show some of that emotional baggage happening on the page. I say 'on the page' to mean something happening now as the reader reads the pages, not as a memory or flashback.

Here's an example that qualifies as a slab of backstory 'telling' on the page: I call it my high school summer dress uniform fiasco of 1982.

---

I'd had a growth spurt towards the end of Year 7. My mother put my reputation through the sewing machine and made my next dress. It would save money! When she'd nearly finished, she asked me if I wanted pockets. Of course I needed pockets, where else would I put my locker key and lunch money? This resulted in her accusing me of making her life 'difficult'.

---

Are you yawning yet? I am, and I'm talking about myself! My favourite subject!

How about this instead:

---

Ebony pulled the teabag out of the cup before the water darkened too much. "Here you go, one weak black tea, not too full."

Mum took it in her tremor–riddled hands and rested it on the bench. "I don't know why we couldn't use the one bag, I don't have it very strong."

"Re–using teabags is scabby."

18

"It saves money."

"Saving money isn't worth it." Ebony played with the tag on hers, watching the colour deepen as she dunked the bag up and down.

"I saved money sewing your school uniform."

"I hated that dress."

"It was perfectly good."

"You made it with the stripes going the wrong way!"

---

In the second example, the scene is taking place in the present, but there's a niggly memory of 'saving money in the past' that caused trauma. So much trauma.

It does take longer to show rather than tell backstory – but if it's important, it belongs in the story, in the here and now, on the page.

Your job as the author is to find a way to seed that important 'past' information into your character's current actions or dialogue on the page (I'm serious about never re-using teabags, PS.) When it's important, you'll find a way to show the readers. If it's not important? Don't put it in the book at all.

BUT HOW DO I GET THAT IMPORTANT BACKSTORY ONTO THE PAGE THEN, HEY? MISSY EXPERT, HOW DO I DO IT???

You write in hints, in a scene with two or more people. In their dialogue and their actions. In a scene where the heroine breaks down and confesses her deepest fears – to another person.

Is there only one person in the scene? Then the scene is in danger of falling in to backstory. Are they walking in to a room and remembering something from the past – in a fair bit of detail? Warning! Warning!

Slab Backstory:

---

'Sarah walked into the room and felt the memories pressing into her soul. The time she was shut in the cupboard, which had led to a lifetime of claustrophobia and fear of the dark. And all her abandonment issues. That's where they'd started. All from a stupid game of hide and seek that had spiralled out of hand. She'd never played that stupid game again and she'd never let her children play it either. It brought back such awful memories.'

---

Hint of backstory:

---

'Sarah walked into the room and felt the memories pressing into her soul. She made a hasty exit and shut the door. Those memories weren't welcome.'

---

A hint is great. It creates interest and a little intrigue and shows the reader that your heroine is a fully fleshed-out person who clearly has a couple of decades of issues under her belt – but you're not going to weigh everything down right now with the whole thing.

Your heroine's life up until now needs to be something of a mystery. If the reader knows everything right from the start, there's nothing left to reveal later on. You're also sucking the fun away for the reader, who loves to work theses things out as she goes along.

**Backstory does not belong at the front of the book.**

"Oh really? Then where can I put the backstory?"

That is up to you.

"Now you tell me?"

The key is to sprinkle in hints and sow seeds as you go, but my general rule of thumb is that you always need so much less than you ever thought. And then halve it.

## LET'S MAKE A LIST.

Write down the 10 most important past events in your character's life that have shaped who they are now. The emotional moments that have given them all their adult baggage. The keys that unlock their deeply held beliefs about the world they live in today. Every time their resilience slipped. Every success. Every failure. Take your time. You may have more than 10 things. That's great. Keep writing. It's an excellent way to get it all out so that you know your character back to front and inside out. This is now your character bible and your source for conflict.

For example, one of your characters had a menagerie growing up, so she brought in every stray bird, dog, cat and bunny.

The other was bitten by a dog as a toddler and spent weeks recovering in hospital. She doesn't remember the incident, but she's grown up with a fear of animals.

You don't need to 'tell' this to the reader, they'll pick it up when you show them snippets on the page. (There's that phrase 'on the page' again.)

Your heroine is walking with a friend and she sees a cat sitting there next to a gate, like he owns the place. She'll go right up to him and rub his neck, while her best friend says, 'Careful, you don't know what he's got.'

That instantly shows you, through their actions and dialogue, that one is an animal lover, and the other clearly is not. No further explanation is needed. No wading into backstory, no trauma or joys. It's there on the page, and it will keep showing up, on the page, building up their backstories as they go along.

Later, much later, when things get complicated, our heroine will finally throw her hands up and scream, 'why do you hate animals so much?' and the other will finally confess, 'Because they nearly killed me!' and it will all make sense.

Ready for your next job?

Awesome!

# THE 'AUTHOR-FILTER-ECTOMY'

## HOW TO RECOGNISE FILTER WORDS AND CUT THEM OUT.

What are these 'filters'? I'll show you so you can see it in your own work. Phrases like:

- She felt
- It seemed
- She looked up and saw . . .

This is the writer telling the reader what the character is doing as seen via the writer. Far better to be more immediate and *show* directly what the character is doing or what is happening on the page. (Whaddya know? It's show don't tell again!)

For example, in my book, *The Girl & The Ghost*, the heroine Morgan Parker is experiencing something of an earthquake.

**Original: "She felt herself sway even though she was sitting still."**

This is a little bland. There's nothing really wrong, but it's not adding much emotion at a time when I want the character off—

balance. If I want the reader to feel what the characters are feeling, I need to get out of my own way.

Filter phrases like 'she felt' at the beginning of sentences have a sneaky habit of letting the author shoe–horn her own observations into the story, instead of being completely in the character's head and letting her character speak first. One or two might go unnoticed, but too many 'filter phrases' will grind your story down.

**New line: "She swayed while sitting still."**

This is so much more immediate and the author (ie, me!) isn't getting in the way of the story.

I'm going through a really old manuscript at the moment and hoo–boy, I am throwing myself all over the words, getting in my own way, falling over myself.

**"She looked over and saw the expressions of agony on people's faces, making her feel as guilty as hell."**

and then a few paragraphs later. **"She'd never felt so alone and worthless."**

What's happening here is that I'm telling the reader how the character feels, rather than letting the character directly show the reader how she's feeling. Fixing it up won't take that much, I promise.

**"The agonised looks on everyone's faces kicked her in the guts."**

Is both shorter and punchier (or kickier) and it's showing, not telling.

The second example? I deleted it entirely.

Your first draft will be full of filter phrases where 'she saw' and 'she felt' and 'she guessed' will feature heavily, and that's OK. That's what early drafts are for. My first drafts are full of them too. I write as fast as I can to get that first draft down, knowing I can edit later. Now that you know what you're looking for, you can spot them, change them and get out of your own way.

Here's another example from an earlier draft of *1916-ish*:

**"Looking up to the sky, she saw it had turned a gunmetal grey."**

Let's tighten that up, shall we?

**"Above them, the sky turned gunmetal grey."**

Or even. **"The sky turned gunmetal grey."**

(Clearly I love the colour of gunmetal, and this is a book set during *The Battle of The Somme*, so it's appropriate.)

Removing these 'filter phrases' increases the pace and immediacy of your story. Your characters are not "looking over and noticing" something happen, things are simply happening.

As you read through your manuscript, reading it out loud along the way, you will find so many more filter phrases. Pause and ask yourself, "Is there a simpler, faster way of *showing* what's going on instead of *telling*?" You will be surprised how many you spot. That's OK, you can curse my name as much as you like, I can't hear you. (I have my fingers in my ears and I'm typing with my nose.)

In first person narratives, there's less opportunity for the author to get in the way of their characters, so if your manuscript is in first person, you've potentially avoided this problem. Go you!

It can still sneak in though, and slow things down, so it's good to be vigilant. That's why you're reading your novel out loud, so you can hear the filter phrases.

Now that you can spot them, you know what to do with them. Into the bin!

OK, let's make more progress on the next page.

# ADVERBS AHOY!

## THE GOOD & THE BAD, AND HOW TO TELL (OR 'SHOW DON'T TELL') THE DIFFERENCE.

So far, we've worked on removing author filters, but there is another kind of filter that can end up being a total pain in the *bleep* to read, especially if you're reading it out loud. These filters are often called adverbs, because they end in 'ly', but not every adverb ends in 'ly' and I'm not hung up on using prescriptive grammar. (I've mellowed SO much!)

Here's an example. Please read the following section out loud. Don't read it in your head first, just read it out loud from the get–go:

---

"Do you think that's true?" Hermione whispered in alarm to Harry and Ron.

"Nothing we can do about it if it is," said Ron gloomily.

"I don't think it's true," said Neville quietly from behind them.

---

Honesty time.

Did you read it out loud?

Did you read it in the right character voices the first time?

Did you read it the right way (ie, with the emotion indicated by the adverb written after the dialogue) the first time?

Please don't send me hate mail.

I adore *Harry Potter* and the stories are wonderful, but let's face it, sometimes the writing isn't. I'm not ripping HP to shreds. I'm using it as an example of times where I tripped over myself reading a book, and I really didn't want to get tripped up.

The example on the previous page merely shows how a reader couldn't have known who was doing the talking, or *how* they were talking, until they reached the end of the sentence – at which point they sometimes had to read the sentence again to get it right, especially if they're reading it out loud to kids and doing all the voices.

I honestly thought that third line of dialogue was Hermione, until it suddenly turned out to be Neville.

Those adverbs and 'end filters' have told us how the sentence should have been read, the reader didn't find out until after they finished reading, which:

1. Breaks the golden rule of show don't tell.
2. Should have been indicated at the start of the sentence, not the end.
3. Kills the pace and enjoyment of the story.

You need to show how everything unfolds, as it unfolds, so that your reader reads it the right way the first time.

Have a go at re-writing this section (It's from *Harry Potter and the Order of the Phoenix*, pages 500–501, JK Rowling) and see what you come up with.

Here's my attempt: Please read this out loud as well.

With a note of alarm in her voice, Hermione whispered to Harry and Ron, "Do you think that's true?"

Gloom settled over the trio. Ron shrugged. "Nothing we can do about it if it is."

Neville snuck in to join them, keeping his voice low, "I don't think it's true."

---

Showing has taken more time than telling. But, did you read this in the right character voices the first time? Did you also read it 'the right way' the first time?

This is not an exercise in having a go at JK Rowling. The whole book wasn't like this – but there were many times adverbs and end filters marred the enjoyment of an otherwise great story. You are not JK Rowling (and neither am I!) so you can't get away with this. (Also, she didn't really get away with this – the first three books were much, much tighter and had barely any 'end filters'.)

What you need to do is remove adverbs and end filters to make the reader understand you the first time, so you don't end up getting in the way of your own story.

In a scene with only one character – especially if it's a first-person narrative – you don't need dialogue tags at all because it's only one person talking/thinking so the tags are redundant.

However, I encourage writers to have many scenes with at least two characters, so you will need tags. You can put the tags at the start of the sentence or the end – but if they're at the end, remember not to tell the reader how it should have been read.

~

Once you've introduced the two characters, and their speech

patterns are as unique as possible, you'll only need tags at the beginning of a dialogue section, and then you won't need that many tags at all.

Bring the tags back in when there's a break in the conversation as they do something, observe the world around them etc, to show who has resumed talking.

With three or more characters in a scene, you will need tags nearly all the time, as it's easy to get confused between who is speaking. Also – don't take it evenly in turns. In real life, when there are a few people in the room, all talking, one or two will dominate, the rest will offer a few words here and there.

A little like this

A, B, A, C, A, B, A, B, D, A, B

This makes the dialogue feel natural, and shows the reader that character A likes to talk. A lot. (Although B got the last word in.)

If the characters speak in even turns, like A, B, C, D; A, B, C, D it feels forced and unnatural.

What you're aiming for is <u>unforced</u> and <u>natural</u>, so the reader can simply enjoy the story without even noticing how it's done.

# GIVING YOUR CHARACTERS
## DISTINCT VOICES

*ecause* you've been so good and you've been reading your whole manuscript out loud, by now you will have all heard yourselves speak 30 'well's at the start of dialogue and probably one hundred 'just's and eleventy dozen 'Oh's.

My guess is every character in your draft will be using these indiscriminately and they'll all end up sounding the same.

Only one character is allowed to begin most of her sentences with 'well . . .' and you'll want to take out most of them because they're all fillers anyway and you don't need them.

Save your 'oh's for when someone else needs to sound sarcastic and they're fed up to the back teeth when they say, 'Oh really?'

Some people do say 'just' a lot. Let one of your characters do this, but not all of them. In real life, most of us do use filler words, but in a book it makes it all a little bland when people end up 'speaking' the same.

Next time you're with a gathering of friends, sit back and listen to the way they talk. The way they really talk. Some of them – we call them non-writers – utterly suck at telling stories. Come on, we all know them. Long–time friends who we love to bits, but they can't tell a story to save themselves. The kind of people who, mid–sentence, we want to say, 'skip to the end'. We're all far too polite, so we never, ever will.

Because you read those four paragraphs in your head and didn't read them out loud, you might not have noticed how many 'alls' were in there. Don't look back, but have a guess how many I used.

Seven.

Isn't that terrible? So lazy of me. 'All' is my favourite filler word. Even when writing comments on social media – I sometimes go back and read over what I've written and edit out the 'alls'.

We all have what's called 'idiolect', the speech patterns we develop over the years depending on our education, socio–economic status, cultural background and pop culture influences. A friend of mine told me, 'you're the only person I know who uses the word 'nefarious'.' I think it was a compliment?

The thing is, we all use words differently and have our favourite go–to descriptions and fall–back phrases. Which means your characters need them as well.

If you want to lose a few days reading up on things, I highly recommend a subject called Forensic Linguistics. It's epic. Everything from the way people write suicide and ransom notes to the use of linguistic evidence in legal proceedings. It's how you can tell if a famous person has tweeted themselves, or if someone is tweeting for them.

I also love Linguistic Gymnastics.

Think about when people are 'caught out' doing something ghastly and they have to apologise.

They deflect, turn things around so that it's up to the recipient to bear the responsibility (ie, the "I'm sorry if I offended you" type of non–pology) or twist and turn things so they don't have to actually say they were responsible.

Like the way people say, "I'm sorry for any offence people might have taken," instead of "I'm sorry for being an insensitive prat."

They also use distancing language, like slipping into passive voice,

ie, "Mistakes were made. . ."

Passive voice is an excellent way to make someone sound like they're trying to pass the buck.

---

Quick Primer on Passive Voice.

If you can put 'by ferrets' at the end of the sentence, it's passive.

Passive is an orphan.

Passive is when nobody wants to claim ownership. 'Mistakes were made (by ferrets).'

Want to create an arrogant character who acts like a victim all the time? Have them slip into passive voice when things get difficult. This is what I did with Duchess Anathea in *The Autumn Palace*.

---

Also, have you ever noticed in real life, people often mishear each other? It happens to me every day. Often with hilarious results. No, I'm not going deaf, it's just life.

But in a movie, people mumble their lines and nobody ever, EVER asks them to repeat themselves. Perhaps because the directors figure we'll pause and rewind if we need to? I have no idea.

It could be fun to do this in a book. As a way of showing a relationship breaking down – because they're not really listening to each other perhaps? – they can mishear each other.

Or – where it works beautifully – your character is so shocked, her brain is loaded with adrenaline and she can't hear what people are saying – just snatches of words, which make no sense.

Have the men sound like men and the women sound like women. In a search engine, look up male phrases and female phrases, and you'll see a difference in language.

Women in the workplace often begin sentences with, 'can I just . . .' while the men say 'let's do this' and other such active–sounding things. Personally, I don't know if this is really the case, I haven't worked in an office for more than a decade.

Keep these ideas in mind as you strive to give each character their own style, their own voice. For example, there's a well–known person who tweets a lot, and his tweets are often written up as news stories. Have a guess who I'm impersonating:

> *"It's a huge account. It's followed bigly. Everyone reads it. Except for the millions of illegal accounts. Sad."*

What fun eh?


You have a lot of work to do:

- You're going to read the whole manuscript out loud, highlight the backstory and delete it. That way the pace will get off to a cracking start and keep right on rocketing along.
- You're going to remove your filter phrases of your character 'looking up' or something 'seeming to be' or 'feeling like'. Happenings will happen, rather than be filtered through a character (ie, the author) first. You'll also indicate how dialogue should be read ahead of the

dialogue, rather than telling the reader how it should
have been read.

- And finally, you're going to make each of your
characters sound different – in some cases just a little,
but a little goes a long way. You're going to Google all
sorts of wonderful things to get the voices in your head
just right.

You're still cross with me, aren't you?

That's fine.

There's that hesitancy, that feeling of resistance in the back of
your mind. You want to create a little 'wriggle room' and only get
rid of *most* of the backstory, not 100% of it. You need *some*, right?

I agree. You do need some. What that 'some' is, is different for
every writer and every book.

The movie *Moana* breaks these rules. I was surprised they
started with so much backstory, featuring their cultural legends. It
was a movie version of a prologue. However, it was utterly vital to
the overall story. It was visually stunning and delightful and showed
us Moana's entranced little baby face while the rest of the kids
fainted and screamed in horror, I loved that.

They got away with it.

There will always be examples of where people 'get away with it'
and break the rules.

Because they're really, really good.

I'm not that good.

I mean, I'm good, but I'm not *Disney good*. Not yet.

The reason I've gone hard on backstory in Part I – and why I
keep mentioning it – is because in my experience backstory is the
single biggest problem writers have, and it's the easiest to fix.

Backstory is like driving a fabulous car with the handbrake on.
You're ready for an adventure but it's dragging.

By taking the backstory out – or as much of it as possible – early on, your manuscript will be in much better shape for the next stage.

Part II is a monumental amount of work, and the less backstory baggage you have going into it, the better it will be for your story.

# PART II

THE 13 MAIN SCENES YOUR ROMANCE
NOVEL NEEDS

# THE STRUCTURE OF ROMANCE NOVELS

In Part II, you are going to fall in love with structure. More specifically, a romance–novel–friendly structure involving 13 major scenes which your romance novel needs in order to satisfy your readers. We'll get there using scene cards, so get yourself a stack from your local newsagent/stationer and some colour markers, because I have a stationery habit and you can too!

**Some might think that structure is formula.** Guess what? It is! But there's a huge difference between formula and *formulaic*!

Formula gives us amazing, creative and entertaining movies like *Romancing The Stone* and *Bridesmaids*.

Formulaic gives us . . . basically everything below 20% on *Rotten Tomatoes*.

This book is all about getting your novel in order by using a scene card formula I've developed and adapted over the years as I've been writing novels. I've taken bits from this structure and that and moulded it into something romance specific, which will keep your romance novel structurally sound. It will help you maintain a good pace and tighten up the soggy middle. It will give you the proper foundations to build something amazing.

- It will show you where you have too much story and too little. You will be able to see it for yourself.
- You'll also see exactly where something needs fixing and you'll have the tools to fix it yourself.

I'm a huge fan of structure, but not all structures apply to the romance genre. The 3–Act model of *The Hero's Journey* for example relies far too much on the *monomyth* structure of the bloke taking on a challenge, returning to a hero's welcome and getting the girl as a prize.

*Save The Cat's* beat sheets are also great, but they're very much focused on screenplays. They're also not *romancey* enough for what we need.

In romance structure, the overwhelming theme is of a heroine discovering her true worth. You know that advertising slogan, *'because I'm worth it'*? It resonates because it speaks to our deepest needs, that despite everything life throws at us, we are worth something. With romance novels, the main characters acknowledge that they too are worth it and they're worthy of being loved.

In romance novels, one of the main themes is the heroine realising her self worth. She is her own prize, not somebody else's prize for the taking. She is not going to sit around and wait for the Hero to come back from his adventures.

Instead, she is an advocate for her own adventure, her self–worth is her own prize and reward *to herself*.

Many romance novels better suit the structure of Kim Hudson's *The Virgin's Promise*. If you haven't read *The Virgin's Promise*, grab yourself a copy, it's available as a paperback and ebook. It's an incredible piece of work.

# USING SCENE CARDS

## CREATING SCENE CARDS FOR YOUR MAGNIFICENT NOVEL.

*B*efore we create the structure, you need to create individual scene cards from your manuscript. Once you've created all the scenes cards, you'll be able to see 'the big picture' of what you have. You can spread the scenes out on the table and gaze at the beauty of it.

Let's write those scenes down!

STEP 1:

Open your manuscript file.

Read through the opening scene in your manuscript.

(I'm going to assume a fair amount of knowledge here. But in a nutshell, a scene is where something happens. The first scene is the first 'happening' in your novel. It may be a little set up, it may be some action, it may be the hero and heroine meeting for the first time. I'll spend more time on individual scenes in Part III *The Staircase of Turning Points*.)

## STEP 2:

After you've read through the first scene of your manuscript, grab an empty index card, write down which characters are in the scene and write a summary of that scene on your card. Keep it as brief as possible. It only needs to make sense to you.

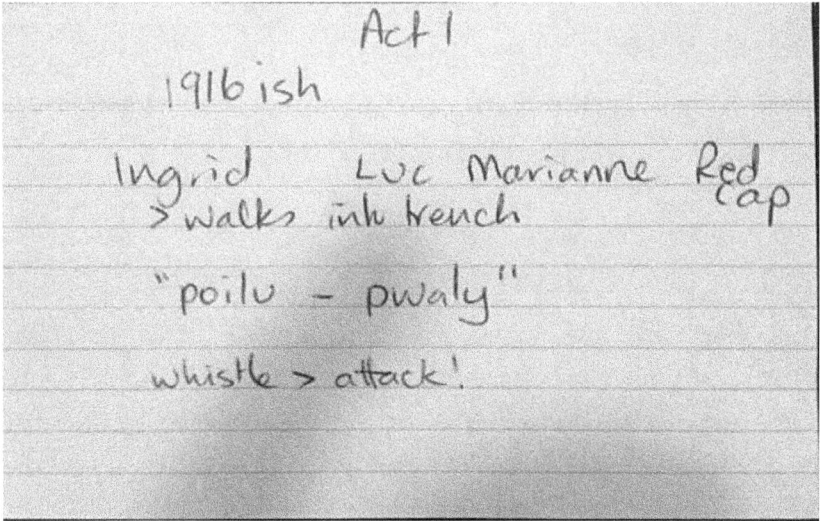

For example, here's my first scene of *1916–ish*. I have the characters of Ingrid, Luc, Marianne and a bloke wearing a red cap. They walk into a trench. There's a whistle, and they launch themselves into a war games re–enactment. (Poilu is a French word, pronounced pwaly, which is merely a reminder note for me about the nickname given to 'the hairy ones', poilu, who were the foot soldiers.) Like I said, it only has to make sense to ourselves, not anyone else.

Plus, look at my pinky finger making a shadow over the card, because I'm a total professional!

STEP 3:

Read the next scene in your manuscript, take another card and write the summary of the next scene on it. You guessed it. You're going to be reading the entire manuscript AGAIN (even though you read through it during Part I and deleted all that backstory.) Write a summary of each scene on its own card. You'll have anywhere from 50 to 200 scene cards, depending on the size of your novel. Bet you're glad you deleted all that backstory now eh?

This process takes a while because you're going through the whole novel, giving each scene its own card. When you do this, manually, slogging it out, you'll want to skip over some scenes. This is a good thing! It means you've found a scene you're not in love with. Ditch it. This will tighten your story even more.

*WARNING WARNING* *CRANKY EDITOR* *RAGE MODE*

During this process, you may find scenes that move the story forward, but are written as a flashback. For example:

---

*Three weeks later, Lisa Sampson sat at her desk, no closer to discovering who had stolen her saxophone. Irritation clawed at her belly at her lack of progress. A few days ago, she'd seen Malhouse hanging around in the tree by her window, talking into a tin can tied to a piece of string. She couldn't see where the string went to. Her dad had then come outside and hollered, and Malhouse had fallen out of the tree and broken his arm. He'd yelled 'sorry Lisa' as he fell. A puzzling development.*

---

Do you know what you've done here? Do you???? You've not only breached the 'show don't tell' rule, you've skipped forward and immediately flashed back to something important. If you do this in your novel, we can't be friends. Not having important events happen *on the page* is the ultimate author betrayal to her reader.

The point of skipping a few weeks ahead is to skip a passage of time where *nothing* interesting at all happens. Jump forward if there's no character development. Skip the dull bits. That's good.

## DON'T SKIP THE GOOD BITS!

Have the good bits happen *on the page*, so the reader can enjoy seeing them play out. If you do find scenes where you've skipped forward only to flash back, it's easy to fix.

Remove the 'three weeks later' or whatever phrase you've used to mark the passage of time, then re–write the scenes as they happen.

Showing something happening is always more work than telling something that happened in the past, but it's worth it.

You're worth it!

At the end of this enormous exercise, you will have every scene of your novel summarised on a card. Which means you'll be able to see the entire story in one glance.

The spread of cards in the next picture shows you what your cards will end up looking like. Your novel will pivot in the middle, and will be pretty well balanced either side of that. It doesn't matter that you can't read what's on each card. I'm doing this to illustrate structure. More specifically, the Three Act Structure (which is actually in five parts, because this is art, not maths.)

## THE 3-ACT STRUCTURE FOR ROMANCE:

- The first column is Act One. Act One is the first 20% of the book.
- The second (wider) column is the first part of Act Two.
- The middle card on its own is the midpoint.
- The next wide column is the second half of Act Two. The entirety of Act Two should be about 60% of your whole book.
- The final column is Act Three, it should be the last 20% of the book.

Initially, my manuscripts look like this next photo.

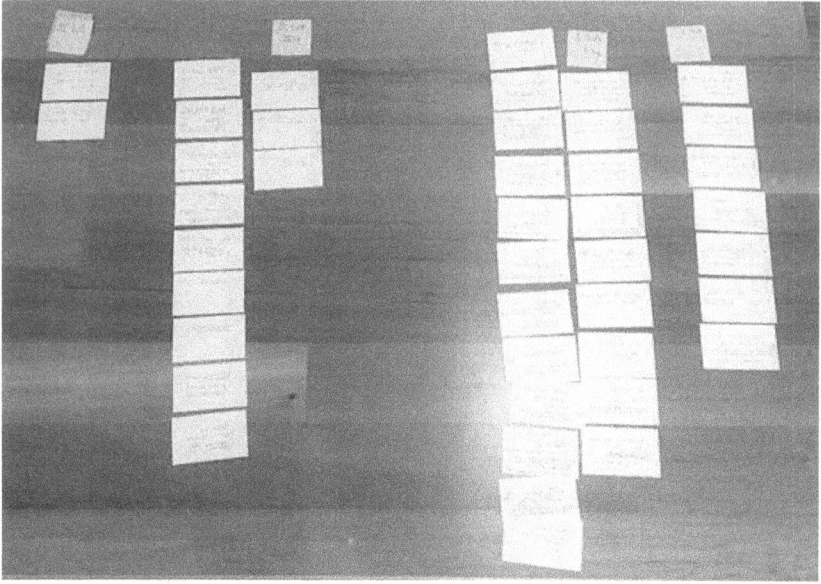

I can clearly see from the few cards in column one, that there is not enough set up. There is also far too much story at the back end. I need more balance. I've rushed the beginning to 'get to the good bits'.

If you have way too many cards at the front end and not enough at the back, it means you've spent too long on set up and probably have too much backstory holding everything back.

But how do you fill the gaps if you're not sure what goes in there? Excellent question. In the next few chapters, you'll make **The 13 Main Scene Cards**, and then you will see exactly where you have too many scenes and where you don't have enough.

Off we go!

# THE MIDPOINT, OPENING IMAGE
## AND CLOSING IMAGE

This is where we need our coloured markers, because you'll want these scene cards to stand out. You'll need 13 new index cards for this part of the exercise. Also, we're not going to start at the beginning. We're going to start right in the middle.

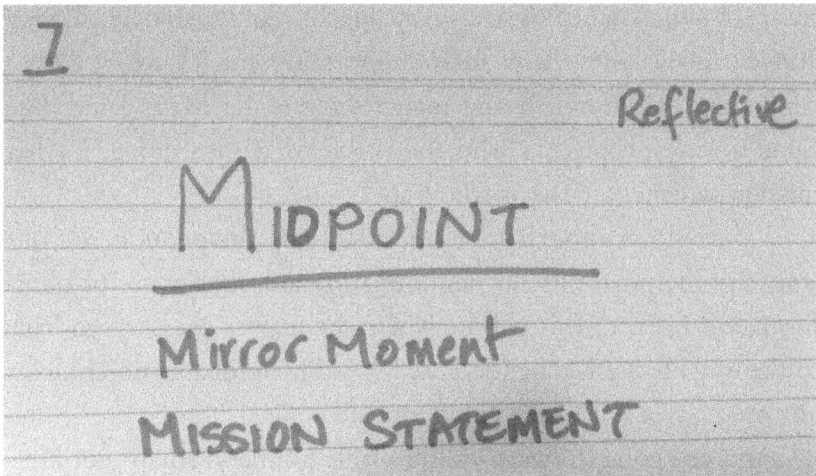

- **Take an index card and grab a marker.**

- **Write the number 7 in the top left corner.**
- **Write the word Reflective in the top right corner.**

This scene, therefore, is where your heroine will be *reflective*. She will reflect on what she's gone through to get to this point, and what she needs to do to keep going from here on.

**In the middle of the card, you can write any of the following words:**

- **Midpoint**
- **Mirror Moment**
- **Mission Statement**
- **No Turning Back**

Whichever word or phrase most resonates with you and your story.

This is the point in your novel that falls right in the middle. It's where the heroine has to stop and reflect – sometimes she'll look in the mirror – and look inside herself. Then she'll decide who she really is and what she's truly capable of. In the movie *Wonder Woman, 2017, (dir. Patty Jenkins)* the midpoint it's where Diana climbs out of the trench and marches across No Man's Land. She came to save people, it's who she is, it's what she's doing. It's her mission statement: "This is who I am."

I can't stress enough how important the midpoint is to your story. It's the pivot of your heroine's story arc. It's a scene of transformation for her. This will be where she realises she can't go back to the way life used to be (because the old life probably doesn't exist any more). She must keep going forward.

And yet, going forward will probably kill her. Perhaps not literally – depending on what kind of romance you're writing – but in the figurative sense or the emotional sense. It's also where, if you've watched loads of classic Hollywood movies, there's an intermission! Because we've reached the Midpoint!

You know in *Gone With The Wind*, 1939, (dir. Victor Fleming) when Scarlett declares as God is her witness, 'I'll never go hungry again,' the music strikes up and it's the intermission. It's a Midpoint!

This is Scarlett's declaration to the world that she can't go back – the old way is burned and destroyed – so she must go on, and woe betide the person who gets in her way.

Here's her full bit:

---

As God is my witness, as God is my witness they're not going to lick me. I'm going to live through this and when it's all over, I'll never be hungry again. No, nor any of my folk. If I have to lie, steal, cheat or kill. As God is my witness, I'll never be hungry again.

---

This is classic foreshadowing as well. Guess what Scarlett does in the second half? She lies, steals, cheats and kills. She shoots a Yankee soldier in the face! OK, it was self-defense, but she said what she meant and she meant what she said.

In a category romance, the midpoint is often where the heroine accepts (or admits) she's fallen hopelessly in love with the hero. She didn't mean to – she probably tried very hard not to – but it's gone and happened now and she can't hide her feelings away like they don't matter.

She often makes some kind of declaration along the lines of, 'He'll probably never love me the way I love him, so I'll just have to have enough love for both of us.'

Does that sound familiar? Excellent!

This is the midpoint for your heroine.

The hero can also have his own midpoint, because I'm all about equality.

I also like to call this moment the 'Mission Statement', because it's where the heroine declares what she's all about – what she needs to achieve to fulfil her deepest desires. As an example, in my novel *1916ish*, three modern–day teenagers get sucked back in time to the first world war – then they discover they're in an alternate world as well, so getting home safely is going to be really tough. (Raise those stakes eh?) The midpoint / mission statement comes when they head off to visit the Eiffel Tower in Paris, but the tower isn't there. The Eiffel Tower is a pretty big thing to miss. Instead of a tower, they find a plaque explaining the tower was sold to Germany for one franc, where it's been re–erected in Bismarkstrasse, Berlin. Because alternate universes will mess you up. Fun history fact: The Eiffel Tower was always designed to be dismantled.

What is my midpoint for *1916-ish*? It's at the end of page 115 out of 230 – smack in the middle. Here's Ingrid's mission statement:

---

*"We might never get home. But we are going to bloody well try. We're going to try everything we can think of and not give up. It won't be easy. In fact, it will probably be terrifying. But we're going to do it, and do it together.*

*I'm done with safe. I'm done with being a passenger. I'm done with hiding in history. We are going home, even if I have to drag Luc and Marianne kicking and screaming all the way with me."*

---

**To summarise:** The midpoint is a moment of reflection, a

change of plans and a desire to do the thing that needs to be done. You take that midpoint and you nail it.

Everything in your story pivots from the midpoint, like a see–saw. You write up to it, and then you write down from it.

## BUT WHAT IF I DON'T HAVE A MIDPOINT?

If you don't know what your novel's midpoint is at this moment, that's OK. That's why the cards work so well – they help you see what is missing from your manuscript. You have Midpoint/Mission Statement card as a placeholder, and you work out the details later. It will come to you. Sleep on it. Ask your heroine lots of questions, especially ask her why she's lying to you about what she really wants. (Don't act so shocked, all characters lie to their authors.)

I mentioned this scene is one of reflection. It doesn't have to be a very long reflection – my example above is two short paragraphs. The Midpoint also doesn't have to be a really long scene either. It will do a lot of work, however, as 'the promise to push on' launches the story into the second half of Act Two.

You'll see as you lay out the rest of the 13 main cards that there aren't many scenes dedicated to reflection. That's because reflection is a lot like backstory – you need to keep it on a tight leash other-wise it will stomp all over the story.

Reflection – when overused – is the author telling the reader to slow down and think about all the events from before.

This goes against one of the fundamentals of story telling, and that is "never give your characters a moment's rest." Reflecting means your character is resting, she's standing or sitting still. As the reader, I'm the one resting, not the character!

## THE OPENING IMAGE

Ready for more scene cards? Off we go!

- **Grab a new blank card**
- **Write 1 in the top left.**
- **Write 'Reactive' in the top right**
- **Write "Opening Image" in the middle somewhere.**

This is a placeholder for your novel's opening image/scene. This opening image shows your heroine at work, rest or play. It's her 'regular world' before things change. Her character is merely reacting to the world around her.

In *1916-ish*, my opening image is of three teens from 2016, walking into the trenches, in a re–enactment of *The Battle of the Somme*, (which was a real battle in France in 1916.) They are at play, pretending to be in a war (which will become very real, very soon). This is their 'normal life' where Luc does not reciprocate Ingrid's crush and she feels he's never going to notice her.

Your opening image will be extra awesome if there's some kind of symbolism in there, a motif that carries through the novel. In *The Girl & The Ghost*, there's a hot pink *chaise longue*. It's hideous, and quite possibly the best prop my characters have ever invented for me. It's there in the opening image and (spoilers) it's there at the end.

The Opening Image is reactive – your character is living in the normal world, therefore she is only able to react to things. Even if life is already tough for your heroine, this is the life she is accustomed to, so she accepts it – even if she doesn't *like* it. Pretty soon she won't be accepting it, and that's when she becomes *active and takes action*. But for now, she can only react to the world around her.

*Romancing The Stone*, 1984 (dir. Robert Zemeckis) cheats and has two opening images. The first is Joan Wilder's imagination as she writes another of her adventurous romance novels. The other opening image is of a classic frump living on her own with her cat, which is a stark contrast to the scene she just wrote in her book. In effect, this visual gag shows us Joan at work and at home and it shows us that while she may be professionally satisfied, she's emotionally very unsatisfied. Not that she's doing anything about it right now – that will come in a few scenes' time when the external conflict (The Call to Adventure) drives her into action.

## THE CLOSING IMAGE

Card 13 comes at the very end of your book. It's the final scene and it's going to mirror the opening image (Card 1). Sneaking back to *Romancing The Stone*, we've just seen how adventurous Joan Wilder's imagination is – and how personally miserable she is in the opening images. In the closing image, she's writing again, but this time she's confident and it's her publisher who is sobbing over the book. Joan is outward–looking now, the street punks who gave her a hard time at the start of the movie are mere street theatre to her now as she laughs them off. And then . . . ohhhhh, there's a yacht parked in the street! And look, it's Jack! He's back! And he's even read her books! Ovaries exploding all over the place!

As for me, the closing image of *1916–ish* reflects the opening. My characters are in the trenches again, but this time our trio are visiting as tourists in the present day, rather than combatants. In *The Girl & The Ghost*, that hot pink chaise is there too.

It's important to make the opening and closing images as organic as possible, and true to the characters, rather than shoe-horning them into a situation because the plot demands it. This is the fundamental difference between formula and *formulaic*. Formula feels natural and gives the readers what they want. Formulaic forces the characters into unnatural situations because the plot says so.

Now that I've talked about the closing image, you need to make a card for it.

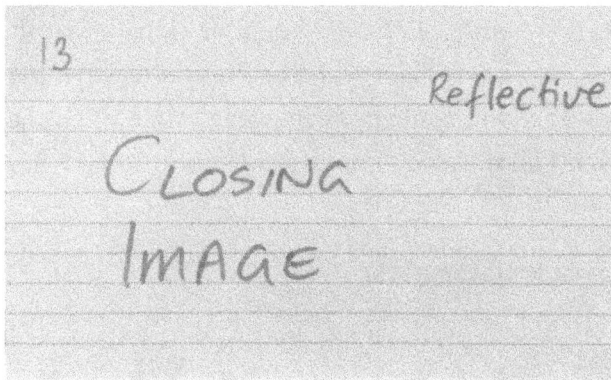

- **Grab another blank card**
- **In the left, call it 13**
- **In the top right, write 'Reflective'**
- **Write "Closing Image" in the middle of the card.**

Even though I've mentioned earlier about making things as

active as possible, this is another (rare) reflective card. Your heroine is at the end of her journey / character arc and she can be reflective. The story is over, she can relax and take stock. By mirroring the opening image, this closing image will show how much your heroine has grown personally.

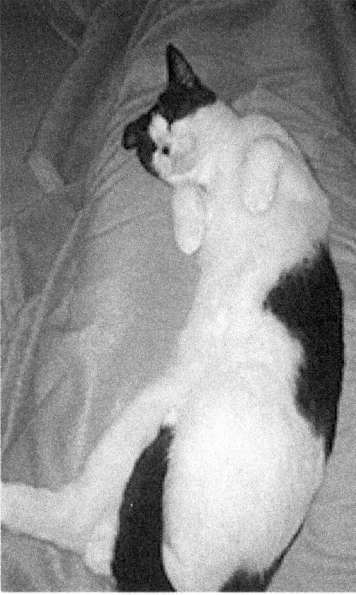

Ahhhhh, another satisfied reader who enjoyed a really well-written happy ending

This is where your Happily Ever After will play out beautifully.

There is no more trauma, crisis or uncertainty. Everything is gorgeous and glorious and the reader will feel wonderfully satisfied because you've let the ending breathe.

OK, so far I've mentioned only 3 out of 13 cards.

One is reactive and the other two are reflective. **Where's the action**?

The action is pretty much everything else, and we have lots of work to do.

# THE DISTURBANCE: STASIS = DEATH

$\mathcal{N}$ow we start get into the plot, which is really exciting.

- **Grab another fresh blank card.**
- **Write "2" in the top left.**
- **Write "Reactive" in the top right.**
- **Then also add 'with active intentions'.**
- **Write "The Disturbance" in the middle.**
- **Under that, write 'Stasis = Death'.**

The Disturbance is the first real 'I can't ignore this' event to upset your heroine's physical/emotional/psychological life. It's a disturbance from her normal, everyday world. Some call it 'The Upset', because something has come along to shake the heroine's normal life. Something is not right.

As the story develops, the disturbance or upset needs to develop into a full–blown threat to your heroine. The threat may not be the end of the entire world, but it *will mean the end of your heroine's world.*

Think about the patron saint of writers, Donald Maass's sage advice: *Make it bad, then make it worse.* How to do this? By giving the bad vibe of The Disturbance / The Upset room to grow and fester into 'the worst thing ever.'

You need to show what kind of threat The Disturbance will grow into, so that it becomes a proper threat to your heroine. Later in your book, you need to make sure the absolute worst thing really does happen to your heroine, which means you need to ask yourself: Is your threat going to be *threatening* enough?

This scene is where you show the beginnings of that threat.

If you're a long–time fan of Dr Who, think about your threat being a Dalek. They turn up and immediately start exterminating people, no questions asked. That is merely the beginning of the threat. Daleks are dangerous. People die. Also, the Doctor turns up and people die. The Doctor is the biggest threat of all, right? OK, that theory is for another book. And this is romance writing and why am I talking Daleks?

Another example – Samuel L Jackson movies.

SPOILERS!

In SLJ's early career, his characters used to die, usually early on in the story. Then as his star rose, his characters made it to the end! But then something really bizarre happened – he was cast in *Deep*

*Blue Sea*, 1999 (dir. Renny Harlin) and part way through the movie, his character became shark bait – mid speech!

Jackson questioned the script, because he felt he was going back to the bad old days of 'I'm the black guy, I don't make it.' Instead, director Renny Harlin told him, 'you need to die, because if Samuel L Jackson can die, anyone can die.'

How's that for a threat?

In *Star Wars A New Hope*, 1977, (dir. George Lucas) we see that the Death Star is not only huge and threatening, it can and will blow up entire planets. So long, Alderaan. It's not just threatening to be awful, it already is awful!

In *Romancing The Stone*, Joan's brother–in–law is dead, chopped into pieces – which is pretty horrible (although there's a great gag about Joan's sister finding 'just the one piece'). That's a massive disturbance. Then Joan's sister is kidnapped and the threat is she might be chopped into pieces as well. Because the threat is real.

Your threat should be seeded in The Disturbance / Upset so that it's ready to fester and grow as the story goes on.

Let's say your romance is set on a farm and the bank is threatening to sell up. Big stress! But it's not really enough if the threat stays at that level.

The love interest can be someone who works for the bank, which will make the conflict fester. (But the threat level is still low.

Then two other farms are sold up the following week, so we see the banks aren't messing around! Your heroine knows her farm will be next! Now the threat is real and it's right on her doorstep.

Perhaps your heroine is working in a big city firm and there's just been a merger with another big city firm. Everyone is worried about their jobs. The big mega boss comes in and she's charming and lovely to everyone. Maybe this won't be so bad after all?

The heroine comes into work the next day only to find half her colleagues have been sacked! Yikes, our heroine might be next!

Another idea: How about a famous royal bachelor who 'loves and leaves them' and has illegitimate sprog all over Europe? The heroine is wary the same fate awaits her, even though she feels all those lovely feelings for him. Maybe he has an undeserved reputation? Maybe she can dismiss this emotional threat? Whoops, he's admitted to fathering *another* illegitimate child and it's only two weeks until the wedding! Does she flee to Paris or go through with the nuptials? Maybe she cries through the entire ceremony?

Whatever the threat, have it play out in full to another (disposable) character so that the heroine can see how bad and real the threat is. Show us that she might be next.

*But wait a minute. Do I really need a threat? What's so bad if there isn't a strong threat?*

Great question!

You might not need such a big threat, as long as it's something deeply personal and essential to life. In *Moulin Rouge*, 2001 (dir. Baz Luhrmann) Christian says he's never fallen in love and doesn't know what it is. How can he write novels if he's never been in love? It's a cute concept and something that calls to our deeper needs. This is more of an existential threat, and it can work really well.

When your threat isn't *threateny* enough, the emotions and stakes have nowhere to go. Your reader will be anticipating something that won't really play out, and she'll be disappointed.

One film where the 'big bad' didn't happen was *The Abyss*, 1989 *(dir. James Cameron)*. The film wasn't the raging success people hoped it would be. Scuttlebut at the time blamed this on people not knowing what an abyss was. I think the real cause is that the word of mouth wasn't strong enough, possibly because the threat wasn't demonstrated, didn't feel *threateny* enough, and it came too late in the story. The threat was from the aliens living in the bottom of an abyss. They created huge tidal waves that hovered over coastal cities *threatening* to crash down and destroy them. But ultimately the waves never crashed. The heroes were heroically talky and talked the aliens down off the proverbial ledge and the tidal waves vanished back into the sea.

This "not a threatening enough threat" is a mistake I made in the early drafts of *The Spring Revolution*. Ondine and Hamish stopped Lord Vincent from taking power. Phew! How lucky eh? Nope. It killed the story. The next draft really hurt to write, but I had to have Lord Vincent taking power and then making life a living hell for everyone in Brugel.

It's not enough to threaten to be bad. You have to show the reader how bad (the situation, the baddie) really is. On the page. Don't hold back. Put it all out there. Your readers will love you for it.

The threat begins with The Disturbance – the first real, tangible upset to your heroine that she pays attention to. It can be hinted at as early as the first line of your novel, by the way.

Like this:

---

"I counted five swastikas spray painted on the sides of the bus stop today. People talk about creeping fascism, but I wouldn't call five swastikas creeping so much as jackbooted marching.

The usual number of swastikas that I see spray painted anywhere in this neighbourhood is none at all."

---

So this opening line marks a disturbance. Something is amiss in the heroine's world. Then when you get to the scenes around Card 2, you can have a BIG DISTURBANCE, where something is not merely strange, it's downright confronting and cannot be ignored.

The Disturbance is often a scene of *external* conflict. How the heroine reacts to it shows is her *internal* conflict.

The Disturbance can be a scene bringing our hero and heroine together. The external conflict is something 'beyond the heroine's control', and is often not a result of her actions or beliefs. *How* she reacts to this *external* conflict will be a result of her deeply held beliefs, and that creates *internal* conflict.

> External conflict brings them together
> Internal conflict keeps them apart.

The Disturbance is reactive, but it's also a time for hinting at forward planning and plotting – your heroine will hint at – or blatantly declare – what she wants out of life. She's having active thoughts. It's also where you set up what the stakes are for your heroine. (Raise the stakes!) What does your heroine want and how awful will her life be if she doesn't reach her goals? This is where the reader starts to care about the heroine as we see her struggling with her situation.

**Likable heroines/heroes**

For decades, there was a general theory that the heroine of a romance had to be 'likeable' in order for the reader to relate to them, to see themselves in her shoes.

It's safe to say we've moved on a little from the purely 'likable' phase to something more ambitious. Merely likable isn't going to cut it. What readers really want is a heroine who (initially) doesn't have what she wants, but through planning, working hard and even failing sometimes (especially failing when her goal is almost in reach) she gets there. Or gets near enough that she is happy with a compromise.

Likeable doesn't mean every other character likes her - but at some level there needs to be respect. We don't want every other character hating her either, as this won't ring true.

When the character struggles and fails a bit but also has a win, the reader becomes interested. 'Nice-nice oops I fell backwards into the solution to my problems' isn't going to cut it. The struggle is the journey and the struggle builds character.

## STASIS = DEATH

This is all about **yearning;** this is where the writer gives us a clue about what the heroine really wants out of life.

Stasis = Death means 'I can't deal with this, I can't go on like this, something has to change or I'll die.' However, the heroine won't be in the right emotional frame of mind to accept she needs to change at this very early stage of the story. She's not ready for personal change, she just wants the *situation around her* to change. Right now, **yearning** is the best she can do.

Psychology time! Human nature is such that when we're faced with a problem, our initial reaction is to ignore it and hope it will go away.

(I did this recently after some rando posted weird messages on my FB author page. At first I ignored it, hoping he'd go away, but then I had to exert some effort and block him. I think that's all I have to do at this point, but if he comes back I'll need to exert even more effort again and possibly report him. But of course, my action in blocking him made me feel bad because I felt I was being rude. That's social conditioning for you.)

The 'death' part of Stasis = Death can be a literal death – if the heroine is in mortal peril – or the death can be psychological or emotional.

For example, in *Romancing The Stone*, Joan Wilder is dying a little inside with every brilliant novel she writes, because no man can live up to her impossible expectations. But also, she's not putting herself 'out there' and dating, because she's at home with her cat, writing up a storm, creating yet more impossibly impossible standards that no man could live up to. (Yet she yearns for her life to change anyway.) She doesn't realise it, but if she keeps going like this, she's going to end up alone. (Not that that's a bad thing, but for a hopeless romantic like Joan, we're given loads of hints that a life without real adventure and romance will be a life half lived.) Also, there are criminals with knives in her apartment, so she's in literal danger of death, although she doesn't know that yet.

Stasis = death is basically a cry from the heart that the heroine (or hero if he's the focus of your novel) can't keep going on like this, something has to change. He or She just doesn't know how to change anything ... yet.

There is a lot going on in this Scene Card. Don't panic, readers are so good at picking up clues that both **The Disturbance** and **Stasis = Death** can be shown with economy and a light touch in the form of subtext, dialogue and hints.

It's also why you needed to remove the backstory weighing your plot down, because backstory doesn't show you what the disturbance is, it doesn't show you the 'stasis = death' equation, because it's all about what went on *before* the story got started.

Like falling dominoes, The Disturbance / Stasis = Death will trip over and knock into the Plot Catalyst (which is the next card).

# PLOT CATALYST: CALL TO ADVENTURE

※

$C$ard 3 leads us into active territory.

- **Card 3**
- **Active (I've written 'Action') but either is fine.**
- **Plot Catalyst/Call to Adventure**

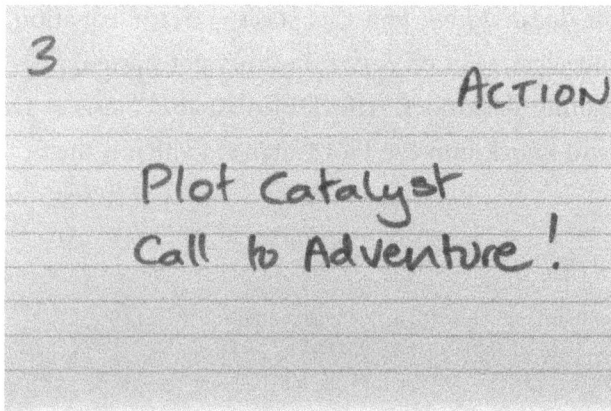

This is the Plot Catalyst, sometimes called the Call to Adventure. Without the Plot Catalyst, there is no story. This card is also the third and final Main Scene of Act One, and the end of this section will launch the story into the start of Act Two.

In a nutshell, the Call to Adventure is the vital moment which launches the story itself. If there were no plot catalyst, there would be no story (or it would be a very different story. Joan Wilder continuing to grow old with her cats, or the criminals slipping in with their knives . . . and she's only found months later by her publisher because the next book is way overdue).

Plot Catalyst is the moment where the heroine accepts her first challenge – her first of many. There will be some initial hesitancy, resistance, or outright refusal before she accepts the challenge, because this too is human nature. We're timid beasties at heart. In the plot structure of The Heroe's Journey, there is a scene called The Refusal which happens straight after the Call to Adventure. But do we need to really have a complete refusal? It can make the heroine (especially a romance heroine) seem wishy-washy, indecisive, as if she's at the mercy of the plot rather than driving it. It's fine to have misgivings and a few nerves as your heroine answers the call to adventure, but outright refusal feels like stalling. The story is just getting going but you're going to step back a little? Nah, push on, I say!

Some famous plot catalysts include:

*Star Wars* – Luke (having demonstrated his desire to become a pilot despite his uncle's pleading for him to remain for 'one more harvest') returns from visiting Obi Wan to find his uncle and aunt burnt to a crisp.

*Romancing The Stone* – Joan Wilder packs up her cat and sets off to Columbia to save her sister.

*Moulin Rouge* – The Unconscious Argentinean falls through the ceiling, suffering a bout of narcolepsy. Christian agrees to step in and write their play, off they go to the Moulin Rouge so they can pitch the story to Harry Zidler and Satine.

The Call to Adventure involves your heroine crossing the threshold (an imaginary doorway, or a real one in the case of *The Lion, The Witch & The Wardrobe*) into the new world of physical, emotional or spiritual adventure.


REMEMBER:

When your heroine accepts the challenge, there's often some bargaining involved, because it's natural to want to have things go your own way. (I prefer bargaining to refusing the call, because it shows the heroine isn't going to simply accept everything that happens to her, she wants things on her terms.)

It's human nature, when faced with a problem, to ignore it or simply hope it goes away. The same goes for your heroine. Early on, she will either ignore her problems or hope they go away.

Joan Wilder is terrfied of the Call to Adventure - the thought of going to Columbia on her own is beyond crazy. Of course she's scared. But her sister is in trouble, she has to do something. There is no room to refuse the call here, instead, she weighs up the situation and absolutely hopes for the best and off she goes.

What if your story is far simpler? A modern day romance that doesn't involve dashing off to the jungles of South America or joining the resistance? Your story could be a much smaller–scale endeavour (although no less emotionally involving for the reader.)

Here are some examples of a heroine 'accepting the call to adventure' but instead of then immediately refusing, she places conditions on what she's willing to do. After all, it's human nature to want things to go your own way.

Remember, every character in your story needs to have their own agenda.

- She agrees to work on a special project with the hero but privately decides she must protect her heart at all costs. (In this case, she's answering the call but also very worried about what might happen.)
- Or she may think, "I don't need a man, but a fling could be fun." (Answering the call with conditions in place.)
- Or, 'He's an infuriating pig, but I have to go along with his wild scheme, so I'm going to be completely professional and not let him get to me."
- Or, "I can't help falling in love with my co–stars. This time will be different, this time I'll be stronger." (She's lying to herself.)

NOTE: There must be an imperative for your heroine to ultimately accept the challenge. Accepting the Call To Adventure needs to be her active decision, so that the story can get underway.

You can't have her saying 'I don't want to be here' all the way through, because the reader will then start thinking they don't want to be there either.

There's a line in the movie *Assassins Creed* 2016 (dir. Justin Kurzel) where Michael Fassbender's character yells, "Will someone tell me what the f–word is going on?" This utterly breaks any kind of audience bond with the characters, because subconsciously, the audience starts wondering the same thing!

*The Da Vinci Code* 2006 (dir. Ron Howard) did something similar with Audrey Tautou's character. She began strong, having all the answers and being clever. Then for no reason at all, her dialogue became filled with lines like, "I don't believe it."

From that moment, I didn't believe it either.

You also can't have your main character being the victim of circumstance all the way through (Thomas Hardy's *Tess of the*

*D'urbevilles* anyone?) The essence of story is character growth. If someone doesn't take an active role in their own destiny and happiness, then they can't grow as a person, can they?

Once your main character has made her mind up, your heroine doesn't merely slide through the 'doorway to adventure', she opens it herself and stomps on through, because these are her first steps on a journey of character growth.

Congratulations, we've created the three main scene cards for ACT One. To balance out the rest of the story, remember to make sure Act One takes up only about 20% of your whole novel.

In movies, the Plot Catalyst / Call to Adventure ideally takes place around the 20–minute mark (no matter how long the movie's run-time). If it takes longer than that, the audience gets restless. If the set up goes on too long, if there's too much back story (which you've deleted anyway!) the sense of frustration in your reader/audience is palpable.

In *The Hobbit, an Unexpected Journey*, 2012 (dir. Peter Jackson) they didn't finish dinner (and all that singing) in Bilbo's house until 38 minutes in. Then Bilbo wakes up and rushes after them, crying out 'wait for me', by which point I wanted to stab myself in the head to let the boredom out.

A few years ago we borrowed a friend's copy of *Cowboys and*

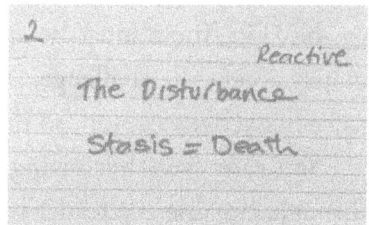

1

*Reactive*

OPENING IMAGE

2

*Reactive*

The Disturbance

Stasis = Death

3

ACTION

Plot Catalyst
Call to Adventure!

*Aliens* 2011 (dir. Jon Favreau). It was so slow I nearly tore my hair out. The pace was glacially bad – then we discovered the BluRay disc only played the extended cut! We stopped the disc and swapped in the DVD version instead. Problem solved! The movie was still terrible, but at least it was fast and terrible, instead of slow and terrible.

In *Red Dog* 2011 (dir. Kriv Stenders) . . . they kept going back to the pub to present time, then the narrator kept interrupting with backstory. I know it's more than 30 minutes of 'larrikin characters' dropping in and out, forward and back, telling us about this amazing dog which is dying on the kitchen floor in the pub. To me it felt like the story only got going when the American adopted the dog, but then I watched it again (for research) and even after the American lets the dog on the bus (after refusing him the first two times – 'refusing the call') they still pulled the story to present day and kept going with narration and 'sit down and listen to this'.

---

**Narration – if there is to be any at all – either has to be brilliant and necessary such as *The Princess Bride*, 1987 (dir. Rob Reiner) or has to stop early on – and can only come back at the very end, like a bookend. (To mirror the opening scene/image!) The essence of story is to show, not tell and narration is the ultimate tell. And a movie is all about show!**

---

I kind of get away with narration in the *Ondine* novels, because they are footnotes. They can be read either during the story, or referred to later. Plus, they're funny.

Also, opening with someone dying is a really tricky thing to pull off. You're asking the reader / viewer to care about someone they haven't met. Then, in order for us to 'meet' the dying person . . . well, we have to go into backstory, don't we?

As much as most of us love animals, a dog dying on the kitchen floor? That's just upsetting. How did this movie make so much money? It was based on a short story and yet it felt so long! And for goodness sake, why did you make a movie about a dead dog? Why am I not in therapy already?

My point is, these opening three main scenes will show your reader that the author knows what she's doing, that she's in control and that she's not going to waste the reader's time. In fact, you will show them through your confident writing and sympathetic heroine with a struggle ahead of her (and if she can't be sympathetic, make her compelling) that the reader is in for a really good time.

The next set of scene cards will confirm that early trust between author and reader.

# STATE THE PLAN

*Let's* launch into Act Two

- **Card 4**
- **Active**
- **State The Plan**

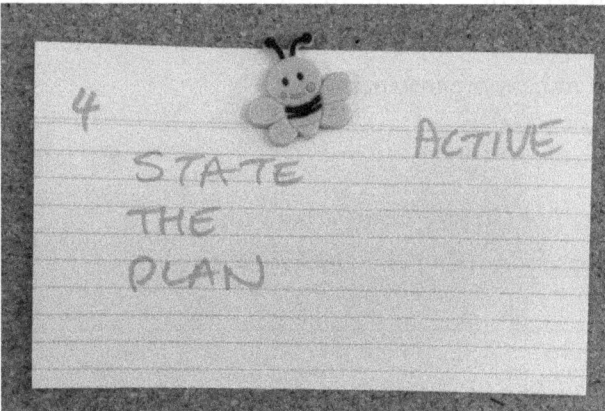

Your heroine (and the hero) need to put their cards on the table and let each other (and therefore the reader) know what they want from this adventure.

(I'm sticking these on the pin board partly so I can get non-shadowy photos, and also because I have these cute bumblebee pins and I couldn't resist.)

This section is known as **'gathering allies'** in male–focussed 3–Act structures like *The Hero's Journey*. For example, in heist movies, it's the moment where they bring the team together and discuss how they're going to rob the bank at Monte Carlo.

In *Star Wars*, Luke and Obi Wan travel to the cantina to recruit Han Solo.

In this romance–friendly structure, it's called *State the Plan*, for the very simple reason that this is where the heroine is going to state her plan. Out loud. It will be there on the page. Whether she says it to herself, her best friend or her love interest, she is going to say it.

By stating the plan, your heroine signals the direction her story is moving in. It also shows the reader that the heroine is taking charge of her life, and is planning how she will face the challenges and potential struggles to come.

Note it's a plan, not just a whim or a dream or a wish that things will get better: "I want to live a better life." Is a wish. We all want that. But it's not a plan, just a desire for better things. The plan needs to be more instructive.

---

*Somewhere Over the Rainbow* is a wish,
but *Follow The Yellow Brick Road* is a plan.

---

(Whoa! I love that line so much, I searched it to make sure I wasn't accidentally ripping someone else off. Huh? It's *mine*? Thanks brain, you came through for me!)

"I want that man suffer for what he did," is a wish with planning elements, because there's an implication that the heroine is going to do something about whatever bad situation she's in.

"He better sleep with one eye open from now on because I'm going to do whatever it takes to make his life hell, starting right now. Beverly, get me a brick and a bag of prawns." Is much stronger. And whoa, I think I went a bit dark there.

The plan, by the way, is what the heroine thinks she needs to make life better, and she will most likely get a rude shock later on when it doesn't work. For example, 'I'm going to work my ass off for that promotion and then I'll be the boss of him!' – so she does work her ass off and she does get the promotion . . . but then she isn't happy because she's still not 'the boss' of her own emotions. She had a flawed plan, and everyone could see the flaw except the heroine. Flawed plans are awesome.

The reader has already seen, from the heroine's attitude, her dialogue and actions, that her plan – getting what she wants – won't ultimately satisfy her. It's like some kind of ingrained author–reader inside knowledge passed down through our DNA. The reader knows the heroine's plan is doomed to fail.

In *Moulin Rouge*, Satine tells Christian she can't fall in love with anyone. Christian says not being able to fall in love is terrible.

Satine counters this withe the ugly truth, "No, being on the street is terrible!"

Their plan, as they sing together on top of the elephant, is to be lovers, even if nothing will keep them together. They can be lovers and feel like heroes and Christian will love Satine and life will be wonderful now they're in each other's lives.

They're falling madly in love, even though Satine knows it's a bad idea – so if they can just be lovers instead, that will be OK, right?

Yeah, we know this is going to end in heartbreak all round. Hehehehehehe, it's a *great* plan!

Stating the plan is classic foreshadowing - letting the reader know the heroine and hero's deep-seated desires and laying out what can and most likely will go wrong.

If things are to come undone later on in the story, the seeds of that undoing need to be sewn here.

# FURTHER COMPLICATIONS

❦

This will be active and also an eency teensy bit reflective, but not much. Because a great writer like you will never give your characters a moment's rest!

This is where you can bring in a little of your previously deleted back story, but don't info dump. Tease it out, sprinkle it through, provide glimpses and hints. Further Complications is where your heroine and hero will clash because of their deeply held beliefs, which in turn creates wonderful internal conflict that provides the engine for your story. We have momentum!

- **Card 5**
- **ACTIVE**
- **Further Complications**

It's where the Heroine and the Hero hit a personal (and possibly professional) hurdle and realise they're going to have to make a fair amount *more* effort to get what they want. Their deeply held beliefs really put a spanner in the works. It's so much more than simply fighting and flirting, back and forth. This is often where writers get stuck – the ones who are really good at starting novels but not finishing them. Because it's often hard to know how to move things forward from here.

Here's how you move the story forward:

Your heroine has previously stated her plan in the State The Plan section. This section – Further Complications – is where we see the first signs of her plan coming undone. The stated goal is not completely unachievable, but your heroine now sees that getting her goal is going to be much more difficult than she previously thought. Further Complications also shows the readers that the plan, as previously stated, won't be good enough to completely resolve the threat (which you have also set up). Your heroine has made a bit of effort, but she's now realising it won't be enough and she needs to make *more* effort. Your regular scene cards might be a little thin on the ground at this point, but that's OK because you can always put more scenes in this section later. Think about your heroine's mid point and what she needs to do to get to that place, emotionally.

# THE PROMISE OF THE PREMISE

❧

*A*nd now we move on to a fun section of the book, which is all about The Promise of the Premise.

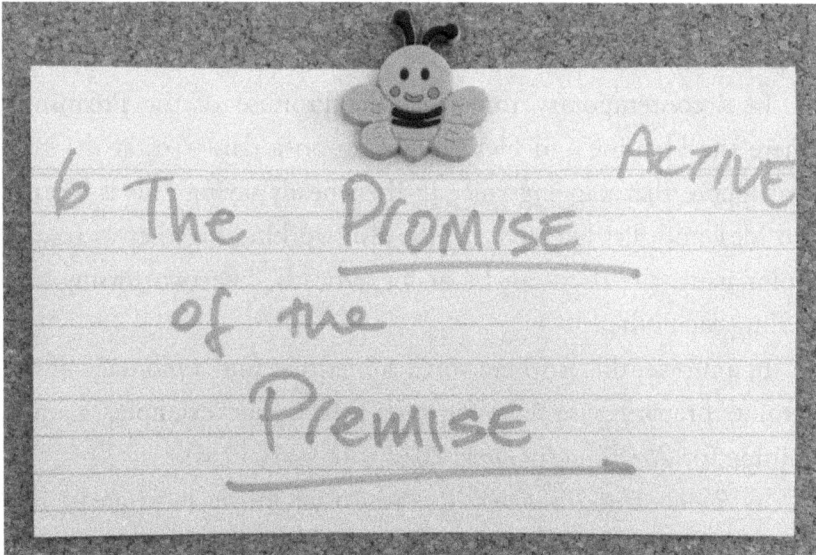

- **Card 6**
- **ACTIVE**
- **ACTIVE**
- **ACTIVE**
- **The Promise of the Premise**

I may have been too subtle, so let me reiterate. This section is going to be ACTIVE! This is what the heart of your book is all about.

In a book set in a finishing school, this is where the heroine learns how to eat cherries delicately, and also walk up and down the length of the library with a book on her head (because she's in a finishing school, you expect that) but it will also be where she's sneakily charging her borrowed phone in the kitchen and absorbing some gossip from the other inmates. I mean, *residents*.

Perhaps you're writing a book about a Medieval gang of outlaws living in the forest? This is the part of the book where they form a gang and come together and start training, getting to know their strengths and weaknesses.

In a contemporary romance, The Promise of the Premise is where the Heroine and Hero might go on a date — or at the very least ignore that nagging voice in their heads saying 'this is a really bad idea' and flirt like crazy whilst also working together to resolve a plot issue. Or they can be at loggerheads, like two hissing cats circling each other.

In a movie, this is where you'll sometimes find a montage of the heroine preparing to take on the world. For example, Katniss training for *The Hunger Games* 2012 (dir. Gary Ross).

In *Romancing The Stone*, (because that movie is so great) this section takes place over several scenes. Joan and Jack are in a plane crash, which plays out beautifully, full of adventure and *the romancing* and the map showing where to find El Corazon (the *stone*). They find their way to a local village – but everyone points a gun at Jack and Joan – until these menacing machos recognise Joan Wilder from her author photograph in her romance novels! The Mega Alpha leader of a gang of outlaws *loves* Joan's books, they're his favourites. The leader then helps them escape when the other crooks turn up. This works so well, because we have the Promise of the Premise AND Further Complications all tied in together.

BONUS FUN, the order of cards 5 and 6 are interchangeable, so you don't have to have further complications before you deliver the promise of the premise if it doesn't feel organic enough.

However, you still need both of these sections – the plot needs to thicken! – otherwise your reader will be shaking her head wondering where the story is going.

The next main scene is your midpoint, which means . . .

We are half way there!

Phew!

The second half of act two is where writers can get really, *really* stuck. You may have a fair idea of what your Black Moment might be, but you're not sure how to get from the Midpoint to the Black Moment.

Some advice will say 'deepen the conflict', but that advice won't show you *how* to deepen it. Which is infuriatingly unhelpful. These next two cards will help you solve that problem. I absolutely love them and I use them all the time.

Let's tighten this soggy middle!

# NEW PLAN

❧

*C*ard 7, The Midpoint, launched the heroine into the second half of Act Two. Now we have card 8, what do we do?

- **Card 8**
- **New Plan**
- **Active.**

Yep, as the previous picture showed, we are having a New Plan, where the heroine makes a new plan (funny that!) and possibly changes or adapts her goals to suit her changed circumstances.

"Wait a minute? She already stated her plan earlier, now she's got a different one?"

Yes – previously stated plans can change along the way – but they are adaptations of the previously stated goal. A new job, new city, new location etc is fine – as long as it's not taking us somewhere completely different to where the story was initially going.

For example, *Moulin Rouge* – Satine's goal is to secure a life with the rich Duke – and this in turn will secure everyone's future as The Duke has invested heavily in the Moulin Rouge building itself.

But oh no! Satine's gone and fallen in love with 'the penniless writer' who she initially thought was The Duke! (Mistaken Identity! Shenanigans!) Satine loves the writer – I don't blame her, it's Ewan McGregor! Her new plan is to keep The Duke happy and make sure he doesn't find out about her trysts with Sexy McWriter Bloke.

Their new plan therefore is *to not get found out.* They keep rehearsing their play – the story keeps changing, they have to keep rehearsing! This new plan includes their special song, *Come What May*, so that no matter what happens, when they sing their special song, they'll know their love is real.

This section of your novel will highlight the new plan and an adapted goal, but the ultimate personal goal, which is evidenced in earlier yearnings, such as security, stability, safety, unconditional love – is still basically the same.

The New Plan is one that will work this time, your heroine is really sure of it! She may need to regather her regular allies about her, or call upon her last reserves of willpower and emotion. She is not going down without a fight! No more reflecting, no more wallowing, she has a new plan and she's going to win!

Note – you generally can't bring in any new allies / characters here. They have to be characters who were already in the story earlier. Otherwise it smacks of deus ex machina which is Latin for *bad writing*.

This change of plan then launches us into loads more action as the story races forward and the plot tightens.

# BAD GUYS CLOSE IN

❧

*I*n a movie, there is often a car chase at this point. In a Marvel Movie, there's a huge battle. (So many battles.) In a romance novel, the heroine starts to come undone, and the undoing is a result of her deeply held beliefs and internal conflicts.

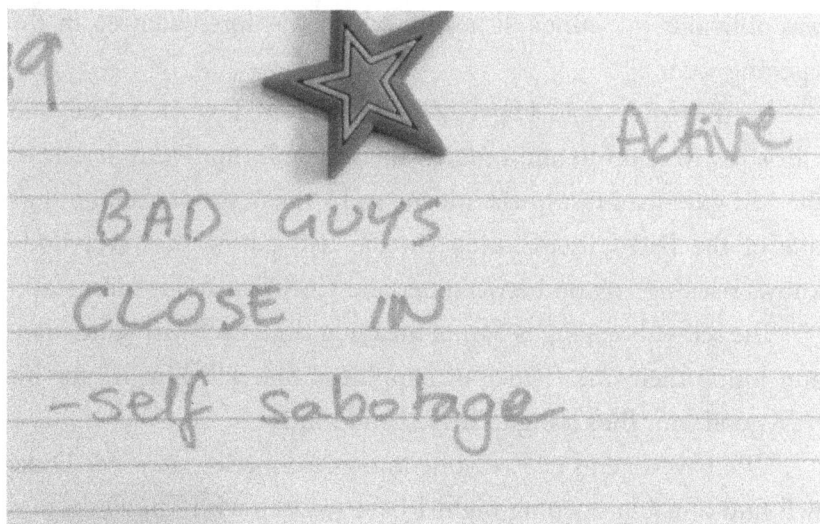

Active

BAD GUYS CLOSE IN

-self sabotage

- **Card 9**
- **Active; (a little reflective)**
- **Bad Guys Close In**
- **Self Sabotage**

Your heroine's moment of personal transformation and transition happened back in the Midpoint. Now we're going to stick the knife in and make life *really* hard for her. Because although she's got a new plan and everything is looking positive, a good writer like you will never give your characters a moment's rest!

In a romance novel, Bad Guys Move In is where the heroine's inner demons threaten to sabotage all her good work. In this instance, the 'bad guys' are the emotional baggage she can't shake. This is where internal conflict drives the hero and heroine apart.

It's also a moment where the heroine is caught in one of those 'this is why I can't have nice things!' moments.

In *Moulin Rouge* this was such a tense part of the film, it absolutely raised the stakes. Up until this point, Christian and Satine thought they could sneak around behind the Duke's back. Christian was oblivious to Satine's ill health, which was foreshadowed in the opening scene.

At the Midpoint, Harry Zidler discovered what Satine and Christian were up to and ordered them to split up. Harry is one of the bad guys for most of the movie, so by this stage of the film, he's one of the Bad Guys Closing In. He tells Satine that everybody knows what's going on between her and Christian and it must stop.

The self–sabotaging is Satine breaking things off with Christian, and losing their one chance of happiness. She tells him it's for his own good (but she's lying to herself and him)/

"We have to end it. Everyone knows. Sooner or later The Duke will find out. On opening night I have to sleep with The Duke and the jealousy will drive you mad."

In your book, this is where your heroine's deeply held beliefs start to unravel, threatening her previously held view of the world. The heroine has a major setback, and her plans, which she's already adjusted along the way, fray at the edges.

Remember back in State the Plan, your heroine stated her plan – and then with Further Complications she had to adjust that plan. In this section, she's close to abandoning that plan altogether. Your heroine may even begin to believe that she's not worth loving. But dammit, she wants that love, she deserves that love. Your heroine may feel like giving up at this point (but we haven't reached the Black Moment either, so she *can't* give up yet).

Your heroine has to keep going, otherwise the metaphorical 'Bad Guys' (or self–sabotage) will win.

In *Gone With The Wind*, the bad guys closing in are literal bad guys. This is where carpetbaggers turn up. Carpetbaggers is a name given to the cashed–up Yankees who arrived in the south after the war, with their carpet bags filled with money I guess, buying up properties and setting themselves up as plantation owners. Jonas Wilkerson offers to buy Tara (the family home) but Scarlett sends him packing.

Jonas doesn't turn up out of nowhere, by the way. He used to be the overseer of Tara at the beginning of the novel, but he got po' white cracker Emmie Slattery pregnant and the O'Hara's sacked him.

When the Bad Guys close in, it has to be with characters you've previously introduced, and the deeply held beliefs the of the heroine have to already be mentioned. We need to have seen her struggle with them before.

This leads neatly to the next important card that will help you pick up the pace and tighten the soggy middle.

# THE TICKING CLOCK (AKA THE IMMOVABLE DEADLINE)

*M*any writers find it difficult to incorporate The Ticking Clock into their novels. The Ticking Clock is not a literal interpretation of a noisy timepiece, but a metaphor. It's where something must be done by a set time, otherwise everything will turn to crap. The clock is ticking, so to speak.

It's an immovable deadline bearing down on your heroine. It's something that needs fixing or doing – by a set time – otherwise everything your heroine has done up until now will be for nothing.

Guess what? I'm terrible at putting The Ticking Clock / The Immovable Deadline into my earlier drafts. But I know how important these scenes are for ratcheting up the tension. It took me ages to get one that worked for *The Girl & The Ghost*. But once I worked it out, it felt completely logical in her family's illogical way.

When you start editing your own novel and being objective about it, you'll see whether the Ticking Clock is fleshed out properly. Without a Ticking Clock / Immovable Deadline, the heroine is merely lurching from one event to the next, and that means she's still reacting to the world around her. By this stage of your manuscript, she needs to be driving the story at full speed.

- **Card 10**
- **ACTIVE**
- **The Ticking Clock**
- **The Deadline**

You don't want your heroine still reacting to other people and events at this stage of the book. Otherwise it can feel aimless and, dare I say it, pointless. The heroine needs to be leading the story, dragging everyone else along with her.

If you don't have a Ticking Clock / Immovable Deadline, sleep on it for a few days, have a good hard think, and then . . . try NOT to think about it. You know how when you look at a star, it's sparkly and gorgeous, and then when you look just to the side of it, it's even brighter? Sometimes when I'm thinking directly about a problem, I'm not seeing the sparkle. So, I'll distract my brain and look to the side for a bit and I might see what I really need to see. (I know there's a scientific explanation for why stars look brighter when you look beside them rather than directly at them, but this is art, so it's a feeling, m'kay?)

It's important that I confess how awful and messy my drafts are – because I'm human and I make mistakes and I forget important parts of the book. But then I go back to these cards and I really do put a scene on each card and then play around with them on the table to see what is missing. It really does help.

OK, enough of me, let's have a look at a really famous ticking clock. If we go back to *Gone With The Wind* for a moment, Scarlett's 'ticking clock' is that she needs $300 to pay the taxes on Tara, otherwise the family home will be sold to Jonas Wilkerson. She's utterly broke. Scarlett gets in her dress made from curtains and pleads for the money from Rhett Butler. And we all know how well that turned out. (I'll go into this in fabulous detail in Part III, because it is an absolute master class in turning points.)

---

*Something must be done, by a set time, otherwise everything will turn to crap.*

---

Another *Moulin Rouge* reference! During rehearsals, Nini Legs In The Air (Caroline O'Connor) makes an idle comment to the Duke (Richard Roxburgh, always a magnificent villain) about the storyline of Christian's play. The story doesn't make sense to Nini; "Why would she leave the Maharajah for the penniless writer? Ooops, I mean *sitar player?*"

Everything is incredibly tense on stage because Nini has just let the metaphorical cat out of the bag. As the players make excuses to the Duke, Christian yells, "Because she doesn't love you!" Then he corrects himself and says, "She doesn't love him."

(This isn't even the black moment. It's gonna get sooooooo much worse.)

Satine realises how crazy things have become. The Duke is going to walk out right now (immovable deadline) and if he does, everyone who works at the Moulin Rouge will be out on the streets. She must stop him!

Also, this is in character for The Duke, he's been waving his money around and using it as a threat against everyone pretty much from the start.

Satine declares she will go to The Duke, tonight, in order to save everyone.

We also have other ticking clocks throughout the movie – the foreshadowing of Satine's death; the contract between Harry and The Duke includes a clause that forces Satine to sleep with The Duke on opening night of the play, *Spectacular Spectacular*. Opening Night is coming!

You can mention a metaphorical ticking clock at the beginning of your book – like a countdown or serious deadline – just make sure you really kick it into gear and turn it up to eleven at this point in the book.

I've used the Ticking Clock / Immovable Deadline device in *1916ish* as well. Ingrid, Luc and Marianne have tried many ways to get back home to their modern time, but all attempts so far have failed. This leads them to believe that the only way back is the way they came – and that's through the battlefields. But this doesn't give them a set time to do it.

Then they find out there's going to be one last train to the frontlines tomorrow morning. (Here's the immovable deadline!) After that train leaves, the French army are going to rip up the tracks to prevent the Germans from driving captured locomotives straight back in to Paris.

Our trio have to be on that train, dressed as soldiers, otherwise they won't get home. This leads to a few really tight scenes where the kids break into their own workplace to steal uniforms, have a run–in with the manager, and Luc and Ingrid share a fraught 'we might die tomorrow' kiss.

Tension GALORE!

If you're writing a category romance, your Ticking Clock / Immovable Deadline scenario will be different, but no less important. The heroine must do X in order to achieve Y result. And it's time sensitive. No mucking about. Hurry, hurry! No, don't race to the airport, it's been done! (So many times) But something like a race to the airport, where an airport is a metaphor for emotional satisfaction.

Deadlines have a way of making people desperate and frazzled. I mean, your characters desperate and frazzled. Not me, nooooooo.

Make your heroine desperate. As a writer, I want your hearts beating out of your chests for this one.

This is where stuff gets real!

If you've read Anne Gracie's *The Spring Bride*, the bad guy tips off the constables so the hero is arrested – then the ticking clock kicks in as the heroine has to find a missing heiress (who is alive and well but in hiding) before the hero is charged with her murder.

It's all so thrilling!

The Ticking Clock is an excellent technique to deliver your heroine and your reader to the real kicker – the Black Moment!

The Ticking Clock gives the heroine (and vicariously the reader) a sense of hope that their goal is achievable. There can be a small victory along the way, so that hope is almost within reach.

And then you're going to rip that hope away in our next big scene, The Black Moment.

# BLACK MOMENT: WHIFF OF DEATH

*T*he heroine is allowed to get reflective here. Good and proper. Go on, bring up all the stuff in her backstory that lead to this point.

The Black Moment is where everything that can go wrong will go wrong. It looks like there's no way out of this.

All is lost.

Love is not enough.

Winning seems impossible from here.

There's a whiff of death in the air.

Plus, in all good writing, the reader always knew the Black Moment was inevitable right from the beginning. It's especially satisfying because this is something the heroine has brought entirely upon herself.

Her actions and beliefs have brought her to this point. From this moment on, the heroine can either fall to bits and run up the white flag of defeat – in which case there is no more story and no satisfying ending – or she can make the supreme effort, dig herself out of this hole she's created and fix it – which will make for an incredibly satisfying ending and your readers will love you for it.

- **Card 11**
- **Reflective**
- **Black Moment**
- **Whiff of Death**

There are so many black moments from books and film to mention. In *Gone With The Wind*, the Black Moment is when the absolute worst thing of all happens. Rhett and Scarlett are in emotional turmoil after Scarlett's miscarriage. They are almost coming back together again and being civil to each other, but it doesn't last. They watch Bonny Blue out riding her horse. She shows off her prowess of jumping while riding side saddle. There's a wild spirit in Bonny Blue, "just like Pa," Scarlett says. Then she realises, Bonny Blue is just like Pa and . . . Bonny Blue takes a horrible fall and dies. It's one of the all time most horrible moments in film. Margaret Mitchell really did make it bad and then made it worse, with the worst thing you could possibly do to a parent.

In *Moulin Rouge*, things are turning to crap as well. Not only is there a black moment and a whiff of death in the air, there's a new threat that comes out of it – The Duke will have Christian killed if he shows up to the theatre.

Satine goes to The Duke to placate him and fulfil her part of the bargain (not that she was there when Harry and The Duke signed the contract!)

Everyone else is stressing out, Christian's heart is breaking. We get the incredible '*El Tango De Roxanne*' medley. The Argentinian sings *Roxanne*, Christian sings his heart out:

---

*His eyes upon your face*
*His hand upon your hand*
*His lips caress your skin*
*It's more than I can stand!*

---

The editing cuts between the tango dancers, Christian singing, and Satine with the Duke. (Jill Billcock is a sensational editor!) Satine tries to go along with it, realises she can't, so The Duke starts assaulting her (because The Duke treats her like a possession, not a person in her own right). Then Chocolat the bodyguard knocks The Duke out cold and carries her to safety. (Chocolat was there in the beginning, he carried Satine to safety after she passed out, so this mirrors the earlier rescue.)

The Duke, as he recovers, demands vengeance – unless the players perform his version of the play, which he has paid for, he'll withdraw his funding - and if Christian dares show up, he'll shoot him.

Harry Zidler begs Satine to be a great actress and send Christian away, once and for all, for his own good, by making him believe she doesn't love him.

Satine, cold sweat across her brow, lungs filling with blood, sobs that she is "A fool to believe. It all ends today."

(PS, magnificent drinking game while watching this movie, drink every time Satine looks into a mirror, or if there's a bird cage on set. You might want to take out an ambulance subscription beforehand.)

Christian's personal black moment, aside from the jealousy driving him mad? He sells his beloved typewriter.

I'm really depressed now. I hope there's something good up next!

# STORMING THE CASTLE

S o very active. All the actives.

Fans of *The Princess* Bride know it's no coincidence that Miracle Max and his wife wave goobye to Westley, Fezzik and Vicini with a friendly, "Have fun storming the castle". This is exactly what they're about to do – they're going to storm the castle.

Is it a literal castle in your novel?

Well done!

Is it a metaphorical castle? Awesome!

This is the last big 'set piece' of your story. Everything is on the line here. There will be a small victory, making the heroine bolder, then a stab of defeat, which sets her back, but then she puts absolutely everything she has in it and she wins the day.

When this final battle is over we can truly believe the heroine and hero have earned their Happy Ever After. They have both worked really hard for it and they're probably a bit exhausted. But not too exhausted for some kissing.

- **Card 12**

- **Storming the Castle**
- **Active**

LET'S SEE THE MOULIN ROUGE SCENE
BREAKDOWN TO ITS END THEN:

Satine's 'storming of the castle' is to put on a show – because The
Show Must Go On – and she performs her heart out. She will give
this her last reserves of strength, and do the very best she can to save
everyone's jobs and protect Christian from The Duke. The Duke is
in the front row, watching her, smiling gruesomely.

Christian's storming is more physical – he's been kicked out of
the Moulin Rouge, so he sneaks back in and climbs the scaffolding
(pursued by The Duke's henchman). What luck, The Unconscious
Argentinean, who heralded the entire adventure by falling through
the ceiling back at the eight–minute mark, succumbs to narcolepsy.
Christian steals his clothes and gets on the stage.

Everyone's storylines converge in this final scene, which plays
out heartbreakingly in public. In a fit of anger, Christian throws his

money (from selling his typewriter) at Satine. He is defeated and heartbroken. So is Satine. Through tears, she tries to reason with him, but he walks away, down the aisle, almost reaching the exit.

From the jaws of defeat, Satine snatches victory, as she sings their secret song, 'Come What May'.

Christian turns around, answers Satine's call with a heartfelt 'Come What May' of his own. They embrace on the stage to rapturous applause. Zidler punches out The Duke, thus redeeming himself. Publicly everything is wonderful.

The curtain falls. Behind the curtain, everything falls apart, but at least Satine died knowing Christian loved her, and Christian also experienced true love himself.

The closing image is Christian on his typewriter, writing his story of the Bohemian revolution: Freedom, Truth, Beauty and Love.

I'm not crying, *you're* crying.

PS, it's not 'a romance' because Satine dies, but it has so many romantic moments.

# BRINGING IT ALL HOME

*G*uess what? You've already done the 13th card, which is the closing image, which lets the story breathe and brings everything full circle.

But we are not done yet.

We are going to set the Main 13 cards out, and match up our existing novel scenes next to each of the 13 Main Scene Cards, so that we can see the 'big picture' of our novel.

I really am making you work huh?

And you LOVE IT!

Spread out your 13 Main Scenes out on the floor or pinned to a board.

Grab your individual scene cards and start placing them around each corresponding Main Scene. You'll possibly have four or five novel scenes around each Main Scene.

This will take a while as you work out whether 'Alice goes to the shops and buys a curry pie' belongs near State The Plan or Further Complications.

Or if it belongs in there at all.

Be ruthless.

I chose the floor to spread the cards out. It was a bad choice, as I managed another shadow pic of my hands and arms. Totes profesh!

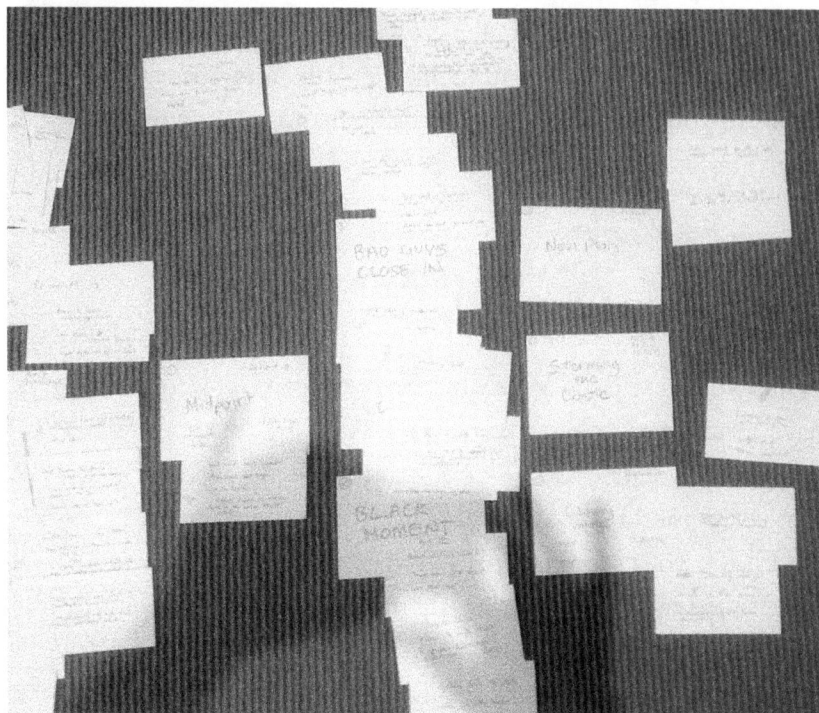

You will have some scenes that must be in there, but they might not fit the description belonging to the 13 Main Cards. This is fine. If it's a logical step from the last scene, leading to the one after it, keep it in. It's perfectly fine to have extra scenes that might not fit neatly into the guidelines, if they are still essential to the story. It often makes for a stronger story.

Remember, these 13 scenes are the main ones you need for a romance structure, but you are allowed to have many more – as long as the end result is still balanced.

You'll also have gaps. This is also fine. Where there's a gap, grab a blank card and write 'midpoint scene here' or whichever scene needs to go in there. Keep making placeholder cards for the areas where there are missing scenes.

Examine the scenes you do have and make sure every scene earns its place. Otherwise, take it out.

Now you're going to number the cards and sequentially stack them, so your opening scene is on the top and your closing scene is on the bottom.


## THIS STACK OF CARDS IS NOW A STACK OF EDITING NOTES.

When you next open your file on your laptop or computer, you'll have a summary of each scene on a card to guide you. When you get to a placeholder scene card – and your manuscript is open at that corresponding point – you'll write in your new scene.

Check your word count as you go, and get that midpoint as close to the middle of your manuscript as you can. If it's out by 500 to 1,000 words, that's OK in a 50,000–word novel. But if it's out by 5,000 words in a 50K novel, your pace will feel way off. Again, the reader most likely won't consciously tick off imaginary Main Scenes in her head, but at some intrinsic level she'll feel as if the story is not quite delivering.

Keep going through the entire novel – this could take a few weeks, but at the very least you now have the cards to guide you through a full edit. You did it all yourself – with a little help from me – and you are in control.

Be awesome!

# PART III

## THE STAIRCASE OF TURNING POINTS

# THE STAIRCASE OF TURNING POINTS

Part three is a technique I developed years ago, sparked in part by reading manga editions of romance novels. These 'comic book' style versions of 50,000-word novels had to be concise and get straight to the point. They had to show character growth and plot developments on the page, with stunning pictures and tight dialogue.

I was impressed with how they did it. If you can get your hands on a manga edition of a romance novel, compare it to the original to see how pared back it is, while also conveying deep emotions required of the genre.

Scenes without turning points kill the pace.

Over the page is a blank worksheet to give you a visual of how this system works, how it will improve your story and make your readers love you *that* much more. The Staircase of Turning Points is all show, not tell. These steps punch home the important moments and pivotal scenes in your story, resulting in maximum satisfaction for your readers (and a warm inner glow for you.)

**Turning Points**
**Blank worksheet**

Every set of staircases, for each character, shows a goal. This is
because in novels, as in life, everyone has an agenda. Everyone is
trying to get what they want.

**GOAL** What does the character want,
and how will she get it?

Remember: Goal, Motivation and Conflict (Debra Dixon). **Goal:** WHAT does your
character want? (short term, mid term, long term). **Motivation:** WHY does
your character want it? **Conflict:** HOW COME they can't get what they want
straight away? (What's stopping them internally / fear / denial etc ) and who is in
their way (externally - laws / culture / obstacles)

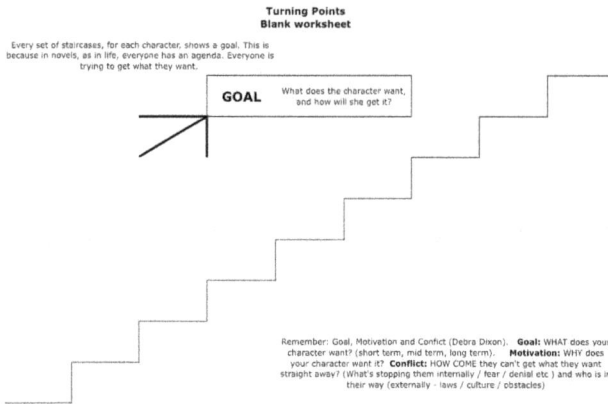

In Part III you will:

- Learn about The Staircase of Turning Points (should I
  trademark that? Just thinking out loud.)
- Use worksheets to apply the Staircase to your
  manuscripts
- Apply well–known stories to the Staircase to see how it
  works in practise.

The staircase shows you how to get your characters to make the
effort they need to ultimately get what they want. You'll be showing
this to your readers on the page (yes, everything important needs to
be on the page!)

The staircase shows the struggle. I had a personal epiphany
while watching season 3 of UnReal. (And clearly I loved seasons 1
and 2 and I'm still loving it.) UnReal is a drama about people
making a reality dating show, *Everlasting*, and exposes the insane
fakery behind true love in the reality tv genre.

Why do I love it? Aren't the characters horrible to each other?
Of course they are, that's part of the fun. But more than that,

they're horrible for good reason. Every character has internal conflict which leaves them compromised and leads the to make terrible life choices. Yet they are believable choices, logical to those characters. Quinn King (played by Constance Zimmer) is sometimes the villain, sometimes the victim. She has depth and hidden wounds which make her behaviour . . . understandable.

What makes UnReal work so well is that every character has an agenda (ie, we all want to get our own way) and has their own goals.

This has the brilliant knock–on effect of conflicting wonderfully with other characters, who also have their own agenda and goals.

In other words - plenty of turning points!

If there are no turning points, there's no emotional development. It will simply be 'plot point a, now we're over here at plot point b.

Romance is all about the emotions and emotional development – which happens through turning points. The readers want to see the emotions developing and building along the way.

---

**SO WHAT THE HECK IS A TURNING POINT? And why do I need a whole staircase of them? Aren't they the same as the 13 Main Scenes and you're making me do even more work?**

---

Glad you asked!

A turning point is one moment of change in the story that marks an alteration in developments – emotional development, plot development etc.

**A turning point is a stage of growth.**

In real life, people don't change very much, but in books they

MUST. That's why we read fiction, to read about people changing and adapting to the world around them and – in the case of romance novels – winning the day with the love of their life.

Multiple turning points on the page show the reader that your heroine or hero is changing, and they're also trying to change the world around them.

Because they are steps, they are very similar to climbing a staircase.

Ready? Cool.

# YOUR FIRST TURNING POINT

he first turning point in your character's development happens early on, very soon after The Disturbance.

For example, in George Orwell's 1984, the opening line contains The Disturbance:

---

*"It was a bright cold day in April and the clocks were striking thirteen."*

---

Immediately a regular reader will think, 'Wait just a minute! That's wrong! Clocks don't strike 13, they strike 12 for noon and then 1 the hour after that.'

They would be right.

It's also not just one clock that's wrong, it's 'the clocks' so we're talking plural – lots of them – and they're synchronised, so it's not merely one clock that's gone 'a bit off', they're all set that way, deliberately.

This indicates something is *very* wrong.

Extra credits if you recognised 13 o'clock is military time (as *1984* is set in a militarised world).

Bonus cookies for those who picked up (and I didn't, I saw this in Cliff's Notes) about various proverbs referencing clocks striking thirteen to "call into question everything previously believed ... the thirteenth stroke of the clock calls into question not only the credibility of itself but of the previous twelve."

The Disturbance is in the opening line. But **the first emotional turning point** for the main character, Winston Smith, is several pages later when he opens a diary with a view to writing his own thoughts into it; an act so subversive in *1984's* political climate, he has a panic attack (an emotional turning point) before he can jot down a single word.

In your novel, that first emotional turning point gives your hero/heroine a glimpse of what life might be like if they depart from the everyday world and head into the new world. It gives them a thrilling (or scary) new taste of adversity or adventure. It's a new challenge or hurdle in their life and the emotional turning point is how they handle it.

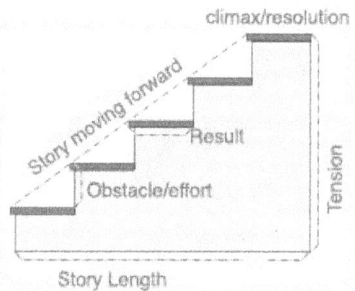

They don't merely take on a new challenge, they do so with fear churning in them, or excitement thrumming in their veins, or butterflies flipping etc.

(It feels counter intuitive to be referencing a dystopian classic when I'm talking about romance novels. However, the most subversive thing Winston Smith can do in *1984* is fall in love, which he does with Julia. Plus, for *some* reason everyone's reading it at the moment.)

If you think of a character's journey as a staircase, the turning points are the vertical rises – where a hero/heroine must rise to each new challenge and get over it.

The horizontal steps or treads are a chance for the character to (briefly) examine whether the effort they put in has achieved their goal, or if they need to do more.

At the beginning of the book, your heroine will be mostly trying to ignore her troubles, hoping they will go away. Later, as she starts to make *a little effort*, she'll be thinking, 'that didn't turn out the way I expected' a fair bit. This is how character development works. Later in their development, things will start to go her way – but there will also be compromises she'll need to agree to as well.

There are many hurdles in your heroine's way and there are several small triumphs along the way too. It's not a solid wall going straight up, and it's not a plateau either. It's a series of increasingly difficult challenges, one after the other, with a few small victories along the way to give her hope. (Because if you fail non-stop and then pull a victory from out of nowhere, it's not satisfying.) It's moving the story up and onwards to a definite point, not wandering around in circles.

There's no time for your heroine to rest until she gets to the top!

There is no specific number of steps – every character's journey will have a different number of steps. If you're writing a longer novel, you'll need more. If you're writing flash fiction or something short, you'll need less.

**Keep the story moving forward.**

**New Task: (because you were enjoying reading that but now it's time to work)**

- On a new document or on a note pad, create three columns.
- In column A jot down in bullet point the major challenges facing your heroine.
- In column B jot down how she overcomes each challenge.
- In column C jot down her emotional state before and after each challenge.

Because your manuscript is reasonably fresh in your mind, column A should be fairly easy to recall. (It's OK if you have gaps, you can fill them in later.)

Columns B and C will be tricker – it involves more work and lots of showing (not telling).

It's OK if you don't have it nailed yet. That's why you're reading a how–to book, so you can learn how to do it.

When you get ready to transpose these onto a new staircase worksheet, you'll put the Column A points on the risers – and Column B on the steps.

Column C becomes your note to yourself, as you edit each turning point in your scene, to make sure you're showing the ups and downs. (Even if they're small, you need to at least hint at them.)

Go ahead and scribble a few of these down. If you're finding the exercise difficult, it probably means you have 'lots of things that happen to the character' but they might not be opportunities for a character's growth.

**They need to become opportunities for your character's emotional growth, which will make them a key turning point.**

For example, if your heroine makes a cup of tea and 'has a think about what she experienced this morning' it's a reflection, not a turning point – unless the reflection leads her to change her behaviour. If that's the case, it is a turning point. However, it's a stronger story if these turning points happen when they're in a scene with two or more characters. That way your character isn't on her own so much. Two or more characters per scene really adds to the dynamics.

---

I often wonder if the reason many writers create scenes where the heroine is by herself having a think, is because we as writers are often by ourselves having a think – and we have such rich interior lives it's natural for us. But it's not satisfying for the reader.

---

The way to turn 'something that happens' into a turning point is by asking:

- **What** does my character want?
- **What** is she willing to do to get it?
- **Why** does she want it?
- **Who** or **What** is stopping her?
- **How** is she going to get it?
- **What** is she going to learn about herself if she gets it?
- **If** she gets it, is it actually what she wants, what she really, *really* wants.

## TURNING POINTS NEED TO MEAN SOMETHING TO THE CHARACTER.

Do you have at least six BIG turning points throughout your story? They need to be challenges and obstacles to your character's journey of self–fulfilment and happiness. Each of these personal challenges becomes the undercurrent of the entire plot.

In *Save The Cat*, Blake Snyder refers to **"The Six Things That Need Fixing."** Your character needs to solve six things, or change six things, or *experience* six things, before they can be where they need to be at the end.

Note – it can always be more than six, especially if it's a longer book. However, don't go overboard either, otherwise the reader will get punch drunk with all the problems your characters have to resolve.

In a romance novel, the six things that need fixing are centred on **emotional needs**. The initial attraction and how they react to it, what they think they should do about it, how they go about it etc.

As Robert McKee says in *Story*, our reaction to most challenges facing us is to initially do nothing (ie, hope it goes away). This is basic human nature (I like hanging out with psychologists). Being faced with a task and ignoring it in the hopes it will go away is incredibly common. Sometimes this even works!

You will see this 'ignore the problem' happening all around you in real life. Especially around tax time when 'you really should make a start on the taxes' but of course most of us do nothing and leave it to another day. Whoops, I'm talking about myself again. Being an adult is hard!

Deep down, we know if we want the very best result, we have to put in the absolute maximum effort. It's exhausting, but the results are worth it.

Using the 'effort scale' a character will do nothing at all, then do a little, then a bit more, then even more. They will have small wins and compromises along the way, which builds and builds throughout the story providing maximum satisfaction for the reader. This will lead to a really satisfying 'happy ending' which romance novels must have in order to be a romance novel.

I'm repeating myself, but this bears repeating. If there's no Happy Ever After, your novel can still be incredibly romantic, but it's not 'a romance novel', and if you promote your book as such, then romance readers are going to be really angry with you because you haven't delivered your promise.

**Before we move on, please fill in as much of Column A, B and C as you can. That way you'll have plenty of items to refer to when you start making your staircases.**

**Then we're going to climb that staircase!**

# THE WIDE SHOT

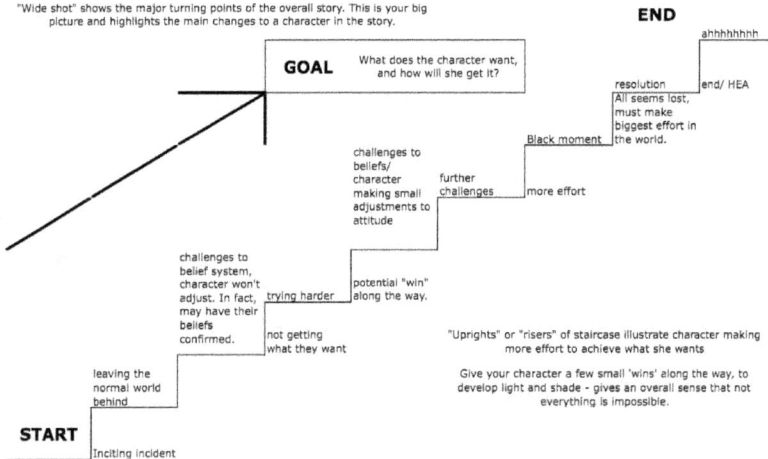

**Turning Points Worksheet 1**
**The "wide shot" big picture**

"Wide shot" shows the major turning points of the overall story. This is your big picture and highlights the main changes to a character in the story.

**END**

ahhhhhhhh

**GOAL** What does the character want, and how will she get it?

resolution    end/ HEA

All seems lost, must make biggest effort in the world.

challenges to beliefs/ character making small adjustments to attitude

further challenges

more effort

Black moment

challenges to belief system, character won't adjust. In fact, may have their beliefs confirmed.

trying harder

potential "win" along the way.

not getting what they want

"Uprights" or "risers" of staircase illustrate character making more effort to achieve what she wants

leaving the normal world behind

Give your character a few small 'wins' along the way, to develop light and shade - gives an overall sense that not everything is impossible.

**START**

Inciting incident

**BONUS:  Each major emotional turning point will then provide the structure for your synopsis!**

114

*T*he best way to use this staircase visual is to see it as a choice of camera angle for filming a movie. You'll have a mix of wide shots, medium shots and close ups. The Wide Shot shows us the big picture of the overall plot. I only have nine steps in the graph to follow, not 13, because this is all that would fit in readable font size. But the overall impression is one of effort, result, more effort, some result, even more effort etc.

The Wide Shot shows your heroine's entire emotional journey.

You can make a separate wide shot for each main character.

Copy the image from the previous page either into a notebook or a spread sheet and start playing with your character's main developmental turning points over the course of the whole novel.

# THE MID SHOT

**Turning Points 2**
**Mid-shot Chapter guide**

"Mid shot" shows development **within a chapter**. Not every chapter will have the same number of turning points or developments, so adjust accordingly.

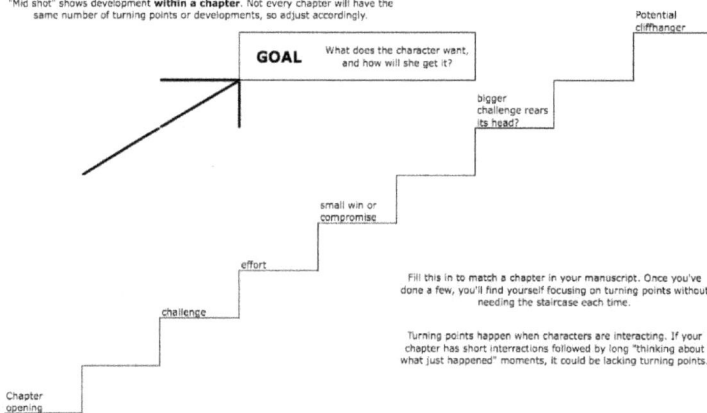

Potential
cliffhanger

**GOAL**    What does the character want, and how will she get it?

bigger
challenge rears
its head?

small win or
compromise

effort

Fill this in to match a chapter in your manuscript. Once you've done a few, you'll find yourself focusing on turning points without needing the staircase each time.

challenge

Turning points happen when characters are interacting. If your chapter has short interactions followed by long "thinking about what just happened" moments, it could be lacking turning points.

Chapter
opening

The mid shot is half way between a wide shot and a close up. Use this for setting out the turning points / plot points / character development that takes place within a few chapters, or even the turning points within one chapter, if the chapter is really kicking goals.

Emotional moments and personal epiphanies go here. Show the effort your heroine needs to make, to get what she wants.

There are no set number of turning points required for the mid shot – but for reader enjoyment and general writing *excellentness*, please have a few.

As you can see, not every step and riser has details on it, because there are no set number of turning points required.

Note the small win or compromise. It's important to have small wins along the way, to give your heroine the courage (and skill set) to keep going. If all she does is get bad news and keeps getting shot down in proverbial flames (or literal ones) she won't have the mental, emotional or physical energy or skills to keep going.

Give her some wins, some small successes, so she keeps going. Give her hope (and then crush it in The Black Moment, because it's the hope that kills ya!)

# THE CLOSE UP

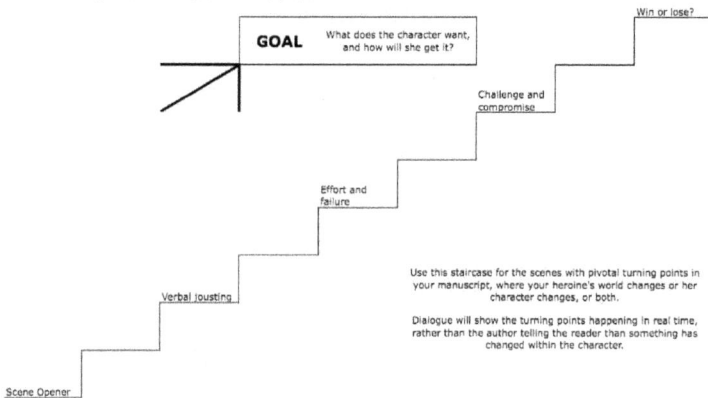

**Turning Points 3**
**The close up scene breakdown.**

"Close Up" will ensure the big moments are fully fleshed out.

Win or lose?

| GOAL | What does the character want, and how will she get it? |

Challenge and compromise

Effort and failure

Use this staircase for the scenes with pivotal turning points in your manuscript, where your heroine's world changes or her character changes, or both.

Verbal Jousting

Dialogue will show the turning points happening in real time, rather than the author telling the reader than something has changed within the character.

Scene Opener

Use The Close Up for your most pivotal scenes, where you really need to ramp up the tension.

The Close Up will work best when you need to show personal

revelations for your heroine which **could fundamentally change who she is and what she wants**.

It doesn't happen in every scene, but it will happen in the most important scenes.

Again, not every single tread or riser has specific detail on it, because close up scenes don't require a set number of turning points.

Somewhere between 5 and 15 is a pretty good ballpark.

Your romance novel needs a balance of wide shots, mid shots and close ups.

Think of the close up as that moment in reality TV, where the contestant is talking about 'her journey' and she's getting to something emotional.

What do the cameras do?

They push in and you see the contestant showing how vulnerable they are. Their eyes well with tears. Their chin wobbles. Their voice cracks. They slow their breathing.

Use it, it works.

OK, ready for the next step?

(This is really easy – you get to kick back and read for a while, while I show you some examples of how The Staircase of Turning Points applies to stories with romantic themes.)

# EXAMPLES OF THE STAIRCASE IN ROMANTIC STORIES

## THE WIDE SHOT

*N*ow it's time for you to kick back and absorb for a while. Give your brain a rest from working so hard and doing all that thinkering.

There will be more work to come, but for now you get to sit back and just read. Because I'm so nice!

Starting off with the Wide Shot – a look at an entire story – let's use a perennial favourite, Cinderella.

## CINDERELLA WIDE SHOT

- **Immediate Goal** – Cinderella wants a better life.
- **Long Term Goal** – security.
- **Backstory** – (barely mentioned ps) mother is already

dead. Father has remarried and brings new wife and her daughters into the family.

- **The Disturbance**: Father dies, leaving Cinderella with her step–mother and step–sisters. (Note to self: Must all YA heroines be orphans?)
- **Early Turning Points**: Now that her father is out of the picture, her step-family show their true colours; they are rude, then mean and then downright cruel.
- **Major Plot Turning Point:** (Equivalent to Call To Adventure) Ball announced – prince giving a ball, will choose a wife at that ball. (The template for reality dating shows!)
- **Emotional Turning Points:** step sisters lose their minds over the chance to snare themselves a prince. Show them becoming meaner and crueller, and Cinderella coping with it.

(NOTE: There is very little information about the prince and his goals, motivations and conflicts. Aside from wanting a wife (to produce heirs), he is there to service the plot, just as his wife will one day service him. But let's not destroy a classic story with over–analysis.)

- **NEW GOAL** – to go to the ball

More emotional turning points:

- Cinderella spends all the time preparing mother and sisters' dresses and has no time to prepare anything for herself.
- Some versions have Cinderella making her own dress in

her 'spare time' or she finds an old dress that belonged to her mother and repurposes that. The step–sisters either laugh at her and say 'you can't wear that' or they rip it to shreds in a fit of jealousy.

- **Massive hurdle:** Cinderella has no dress, can't go to the ball. This is a fairy tale, so Cinderella wishes and dreams and her Fairy God Mother shows up and fixes everything. BUT – **Cinderella's victory comes with a compromise** – she must leave the ball at midnight.

In modern romances, we want the heroines to be advocates for their own story, so they find the 'Fairy God Mother within', who grants them permission to be awesome and *get the good thing*.

I'm writing a version of Cinderella where she makes her own (modest) dress and walks to the ball. She deliberately walks through the forest, her dress catching on spider web silk, making it glisten in the moonlight. She looks amazing. Also, there is only candlelight in the ballroom, so people don't see too much detail, only the glistening and sparkles. Later, a spider crawls out of her hair and people freak out, chasing her from the ball and she runs away.

- **Turning Point:** Cinderella arrives at the palace ballroom. Her efforts have worked, she dances all night with the prince. He instantly falls in love with her (or at least her child–bearing hips)

**The Midpoint:**

- Midnight! Horror!!!!!
- Cinderella races off because she made a promise to her

122

fairy godmother that she would, and Cinderella always keeps her promise.

- Leaves one shoe behind
- Prince searches for her

- **The Bad Guys Close In:**

Step sisters lock Cinderella away, pretend she doesn't exist. Prince can't hear Cinderella calling for help. Emotional turning point: Her emotions are at rock bottom, but she's determined to break out.

- **Ticking Clock/Immovable Deadline:**

Cinderella must escape her locked room before the Prince leaves, taking the other shoe with him, never to return. This is her one chance of happiness.

She breaks free and appears before The Prince (who . . . I dunno, he doesn't recognise her? The hell? This is *messed up*!). Her emotions are twirling and whirling and she's full of hope and wonder.

Give them hope. It's the hope that leads so perfectly to The Black Moment.

- **Black Moment:**

Step sisters break the shoe!

Oh noes! Devastations! How will Cinderella ever prove she's who she says she is (and now I think about it, why would she want to marry a bloke who is so hung up on appearances he doesn't even recognise his one true love in her regular clothes?)

- **Storming the Castle:**

Cinderella has the other shoe – she had it all along.

Yeah, I know, totally lame 'storming the castle'.

It does show that Cinderella had a little determination in her, that she had the sense to keep the other shoe, just in case. She might have had the Fairy God Mother to help out earlier, but when the crunch came she was the agent of her own happiness after all.

- **Happy Ever After**

By the end of the story, Cinderella has achieved her goals of a better life and security. She also has extra things she probably didn't even realise were goals in the beginning but are just as important: True love, security and happy ever after.

~

THE MID SHOT

**The mid–shot includes several scenes over the space of a few chapters.**

**Example: *Gone With The Wind* (novel (hideously racist) and movie (still really bad) ) – by Margaret Mitchell**

GOAL – Scarlett needs $300 to pay the taxes on Tara.

She has no money. Everyone is broke. If Scarlett doesn't pay up, not only will her family be cast out of Tara, but their former overseer Jonas Wilkerson and his "white trash" wife Emmie Slattery will buy Tara for pennies in the dollar. (So there's an immovable deadline.)

Rhett Butler is the only one around with money. Rumour has

it, he's made a personal fortune from speculating and smuggling goods through the blockades during the war.

Scarlett is going to beg him for money. Offering *whatever it takes* to secure Tara's future.

BUT! Scarlett can't turn up to Rhett in her rags. She has to look like she's not COMPLETELY desperate. Even though she is.

---

> *"She saw Ellen's moss–green velvet carpet, now worn and scuffed and torn and spotted from the numberless men who had slept upon it, and the sight depressed her more, for it made her realize that Tara was just as ragged as she."*

---

DEPRESSED:

Looks out window, leans against curtains with a sigh –

IDEA!

Gets curtains down to make dress.

STUMBLING BLOCK

Mammy refuses to help make the dress.

*"Ain' no reason why Miss Ellen's chile kain weah rags ef she wants ter, n'eve'ybody respec' her lak she wo' silk."*

EFFORT:

But they must pay the taxes on Tara.

---

> *"Are you going to argue with me about a little matter of Mother's curtains when that trash Emmie Slattery who killed Mother is fixing to move into this house and sleep in the bed Mother slept in?"*

---

(Note: Emmie Slattery didn't directly kill Scarlett's mother. Instead, Scarlett's Ma tended many sick people with typhoid, and Emmie was one of them. Not that Scarlett cares, she's so fuelled with burning resentment she'll happily blame Emmie.)

STUMBLING BLOCK

Mammy is still suspicious about Scarlett's motivations.

Scarlett can't make eye contact with her (avoidance)

Mammy agrees to help make the dress – but demands that she gets to come to Atlanta too. (compromise)

EFFORT:

Scarlett tries persuasion, says that Mammy already runs Tara and is needed at home, Scarlett will be fine in Atlanta on her own.

STUMBLING BLOCK

When Mammy says she's going to Atlanta, she's going to Atlanta, case closed!

---

VICTORY/COMPROMISE

Scarlett will get her dress, but must *compromise* and take Mammy to Atlanta with her.

---

(So here we already have a battle to simply get the dress, much less everything else Scarlett needs to do to get that $300.)

BIGGER PICTURE TURNING POINT: (in the novel, but not included in the movie) While making the dress, everyone at Tara is laughing and acting as if they're going to a ball. Only Scarlett knows the true desperation of their circumstances, and **resentment towards everyone – except Ashley – grows.**

Scarlett is still opportunistic and hopes to smile her way through troubles and mistakes, but the world is changing and so is she. She is becoming harder and more brittle. Everyone else belongs to some other world that doesn't exist anymore. The war took that away. **Now it's time to adapt or die.**

SCARLETT AND MAMMY IN ATLANTA

Atlanta is mud and cinders from war damage. BUT new buildings are going up all over the place. There's a vibrancy and sense of renewal in the air. So many new names on storefronts too.

STUMBLING BLOCK

**Rhett Butler is in jail.** Scarlett has come to Atlanta to "borrow" money from Rhett/become his mistress. Being in jail makes that very difficult. BUT it might also be an opportunity.

IDEA:

---

*"If she could somehow manage to marry him **while he was in jail**, all those millions would be hers and hers alone should he be executed.*

*And if marriage was not possible, perhaps she could get a loan from him by promising to marry him when he was released or by promising—oh promising anything! And if they hanged him, her day of settlement would never come."*

---

VICTORY: It's important to have some small 'wins' along the way.

When Scarlett gets to see Rhett, he is excited to see her.

Scarlett tells Rhett some fibs about how fabulous everything is at Tara.

Rhett is having some personal turning points too – he starts to believe Scarlett may love him back at long last!

STUMBLING BLOCK: Rhett sees through her disguise (ie, her callused hands) and her desperation.

FAILURE! Rhett couldn't give her the money anyway; his funds are locked away in Liverpool.

Scarlett is furious! All that effort for nothing!

NEW PLAN – as Scarlett is growing ever more desperate to get $300. Who should come by but Frank Kennedy! Frank has a store that is doing well. He's also thinking of expanding the business and buying a lumber mill.

Frank is really Suellen's beau (Suellen is Scarlett's sister), but Suellen is a meanie who hates Tara. If Scarlett 'lets' Frank marry her sister, Suellen will probably abandon Tara and the rest of the family, and be a total pain into the bargain.

GOAL

Scarlett needs Frank's money!

EFFORT

Scarlett marries Frank Kennedy!

RESULT!!!!!!

Scarlett writes a cheque for $300 and saves Tara.

COMPROMISE – she's married to Frank now and she and must live in Atlanta to build the business and secure their financial future.

Personal turning points that soon follow:

- the more money Scarlett has, the more the Yankees can take from her.
- Having money is what she wanted, but now that she has it, it's made her hard.
- She used to think if she had money she'd be able to relax, but the more money she has, the more she can lose.

USING THE BIG PICTURE WIDE SHOT AND THE MID SHOT:

- Use them when you first have the spark of an idea for a book. It will help show you where your characters need to be going – and will give them a direction to follow.
- Use it after you're a few chapters in, especially if you're hitting the soggy middle and you're not sure where to go.
- Use it when you've finished a draft and you need to see the 'bigger picture'
- Use it when you've picked out an old manuscript from the bottom drawer and you're wondering if you can salvage it.
- Use it to polish your manuscript to a shining lustre!

**One thing that will happen:** Your turning points, and there-fore all your forward momentum, will happen **on the page.**

**Your scenes where the characters have a cup of tea, or talk over / think over things that have happened in the past won't make it into the final story.**

**This is a good thing.**

And another thing.

**With the staircase, you will see that when a character has a small victory, it often comes with a further obstacle or compromise.**

Now, let's move on to the Close Up.

~

THE CLOSE UP!

**This is where you can really power up your novel, putting a whole staircase of turning points within one really powerful scene.**

129

One of my all time favourite movies is *Victor/Victoria 1982* (dir. Blake Edwards). It's a lovely, proper romance, full of people pretending to be what they're not and being more successful as a fake than as a real person.

There's a marvellous scene where Victoria, living as a man who is a successful female impersonator, has fallen completely in love with King, a tough Chicago gangster. They both have public personas they must maintain, in order to remain successful. But keeping their private lives private is proving a terrible stumbling block:

In this scene, King's macho bodyguard accidentally interrupts King and Victoria in bed - and the bodygard thinks his boss is gay. (This in turn leads to the bodyguard coming out.)

Action!

*King: Places the broken door over the door way.*

Victoria - What's wrong?

King: - Nothing, nothing. I'm finding this trip to Paris a little more...bizarre than usual.

V: Thanks a lot.

K: - Not you. No, not you.

V: - Why not me? I mean, a woman pretending to be man pretending to be...

K: - Well, you can stop pretending.

*(Turning point, King wants Victoria to stop doing the very thing that's made her successful.)*

V: - And do what?

K: Be yourself.

V: And what's that?

K: What do you mean? You're a woman in love with a man.

V: - Yes?

K: (confused) - Are we communicating?

V: You said, "A woman in love with a man," but you didn't finish.

K: Okay. What's the finish?

V: A woman in love with a man, pretending to be a man...

K: - I said, "You can stop pretending."

V: But, you see, I don't think I want to. I'm a big star now. I'm a success.

*(Stumbling blocks - their career goals are at odd with their personal goals)*

K: Oh, that.

*(How dismissive! Bad King, Bad King!)*

V: And something more. I find it all really fascinating. I mean, there are things available to me as a man...that I could never have as a woman - I'm emancipated.

K: - Emancipated?

V: Well, I'm my own man, so to speak. You should be able to relate to that.

K: To be honest with you, I'm having a little trouble relating to anything.

V: Look, If we'll have any kind of future together it's important that you understand.

K: I want to understand.

V: Would it be fair for me to ask you to give up your job?

K: - It'd be ridiculous.

V: - But you expect me to give up mine.

K: There's a difference, for Christ's sake!

V: - Right, but there shouldn't be.

*(This is all playing out so painfully. I ADORE when the hero and heroine talk over their issues and still can't resolve them. This is so satisfying for a reader.)*

K: Well, look, I'm not the one pretending to be someone else. Let's put the shoe on the other foot. Let's say that you're a man, and I'm a woman pretending to be a man.

V: I think it would depend a lot on why you were pretending.

K: Come on now Victoria you said, it's important that I understand. It's important that you understand, too.

V: - Sure.

K: Love is a two-way street. Why did I say that?

V: - I don't know, but what's your point?

K: You said, if we were going to have any kind of future...

V: Well, what do you mean by future?

K: - We'll live together?

V: - Possibly.

K: - Sleep together?

V: - Hopefully.

K: While you keep on working?

V: - Yes.

K: - Pretending to be a man.

V: If I didn't, I wouldn't have a job.

*(This breaks my heart every time! Why should Victoria have to give up her job? She's really good at it!)*

K: And while we're living and sleeping together, what's everybody going to think?

V: I guess they're going to think that you're living and sleeping with a man.

K: - How do you feel about that?

V: - They'll think the same about me!

K: - But you're a woman.

V: - Yeah but they don't know.

K: You do.

V: And you know you're a man! I don't see the difference.

K: We'll be living a damned lie.

V: I don't think that's what's really bothering you.

*(Again, they're talking about their issues and the tension is getting even worse, rather than getting better. What fabulous stumbling blocks!)*

K: Well, if you think I'm worried about everybody thinking I'm a fag, you're right.

V: So, we have a problem.

K: I guess we have.

V: Well, it's probably for the best.

K: That's as bad as, "Love is a two-way street."

V: What it lacks in originality, it makes up for in prophecy. Eventually, I'd ask you to stop being a gangster...because I was worried about everyone thinking I was your moll.

K: I am not a gangster.

V: Just a businessman with a bodyguard.

K: A businessman who does business with gangsters...and doesn't have a bodyguard is soon out of business.

V: A businessman who does business with gangsters...and pretends he's not a gangster sounds like the kind of act I do. I think we're both pretenders. And that's not a very good basis for a relationship. But it was fun while it lasted.

～

So, how brilliant was that scene? It's a lovely close up scene of the hero and heroine talking over their issues and being unable to resolve them. The turning points are right there on the screen, showing us what a hard time they're having.

The scene begins with Victoria in a jovial mood and King confused, it ends with King laying down the law about her work and Victoria being willing to walk away. High emotions indeed.

On the whole, Victor/Victoria is a charming movie but it's missing a few vital scenes. Such as a scene where King and Victoria admit they love each other. That is kind of important. In the end, Victoria compromises and gives up her job to be with King, and King compromises and sells out his share of his Chicago club.

～

Let's move on to one of the most famous scenes in cinema, and it's packed with turning points. It's the famous scene from *Gone With The Wind* where Scarlett visits Rhett in jail.

The first half of the movie and book has shown us Scarlett always wants her own way and often lies to get what she wants. As we all know, when someone lies, they have to keep lying.

In this Close Up, we know Scarlett's goal is to get $300 from Rhett, by fair means or foul.

In the film and the book, Scarlett has an immediate small victory – Rhett is genuinely pleased to see her. This is an achievement, and it boosts Scarlett's ego – she thinks her plan is working!

Scarlett won't let Rhett kiss her *properly*. She's flirting and playing coy, because this is how she's always behaved with men. AND she still hasn't completely forgiven him for abandoning them on the roadside to go off and fight for the Confederacy

EDIT YOUR OWN ROMANCE NOVEL

(This is when Melanie had just given birth and Atlanta had fallen.)

Here is a beautiful piece from the novel:

---

Rhett says: *"Southerners can never resist a losing cause. But never mind my reasons. It's enough that I'm forgiven."*
Scarlett: *"You're not. I think you're a hound."*
*But she caressed the last word until it might have been "darling."*

---

Rhett also admits that during his time away, he thought of her often.

**VICTORY:** Scarlett thinks Rhett's in love with her and will do whatever she wants.

**STUMBLING BLOCK:** Scarlett is afraid her true emotions / desperation will show on her face.

**MORE EFFORT:** She must hide her true feelings and keep lying to him, to the point where she starts believing her own lies:

---

*In a moment I'll be crying, she thought in a frenzy of wonder and excitement. Shall I let myself cry? Would that seem more natural?*

---

To Scarlett, it feels as if Rhett is about to confess his true feelings after all – he's so happy to see her and so pleasant and kind; he might be about to admit he loves her. (Personally I think he really does love Scarlett, that's why he's so cruel to her later, because he let himself fall for her, thinking she'd be able to love him in return.)

**VICTORY:** Rhett kisses her hands only to see ...
**STUMBLING BLOCK:** ... the calluses on her hands!
Scarlett's lie is exposed!

---

Rhett: *"So you have been doing very nicely at Tara, have you? Cleared so much money on the cotton you can go visiting. What have you been doing with your hands—plowing?"*

*She tried to wrench them away but he held them hard, running his thumbs over the calluses.*

*"These are not the hands of a lady," he said and tossed them into her lap.*

---

**ROADBLOCK:** Victory feels completely out of reach. But Scarlett is not done yet.

---

*I didn't realize my hands looked so bad. Of course, he would notice them. And now I've lost my temper and probably ruined everything. Oh, to have this happen when he was right at the point of a declaration!*

---

More effort: (another lie!)

---

*"I think you're real rude to throw off on my poor hands. Just because I went riding last week without my gloves and ruined them—"*

---

**ROADBLOCK:**

Rhett calls her on it. He knows she's lying. Now that she's letting her emotions out, Scarlett admits she doesn't care if he hangs!

Rhett:

---

*"What a gambler you are, Scarlett," he jeered. "You took a chance that my incarceration away from female companionship would put me in such a state I'd snap at you like a trout at a worm."*

*And that's what you did, thought Scarlett with inward rage, and if it hadn't been for my hands—*

---

Rhett:

---

*"See if you can **tell me the truth** about why you wanted to lead me into wedlock."*

---

Another chance at victory. **MORE EFFORT**:
(effort, block; effort, block)

---

*There was a suave, almost teasing note in his voice and she took heart. Perhaps everything wasn't lost, after all. Of course, she had ruined any hope of **marriage** but, even in her despair, she was glad. There was something about this immobile man which frightened her, so that now the thought of marrying him was fearful. But perhaps if she was clever and played on his* *sympathies and his memories, she could secure a loan. She pulled her face into a placating and childlike expression.*

*"Oh, Rhett, you can help me so much—if you'll just be sweet."*

*"There's nothing I like better than being—sweet."*

*"Rhett, for old friendship's sake, I want you to do me a favor."*

*"So, at last the horny–handed lady comes to her real mission. I feared that 'visiting the sick and the imprisoned' was not your proper role. What do you want? Money?"*

*The bluntness of his question ruined all hopes of leading up to the matter in any circuitous and sentimental way. "Don't be mean, Rhett," she coaxed. "I do want some money.*

*I want you to lend me three hundred dollars."*

*"The truth at last. Talking love and thinking money. How truly feminine! Do you need the money badly?"*

*"Oh, ye— Well,* **not so terribly but I could use it."**

---

**And so we see here that Scarlett is *still* lying.**
Rhett:

---

*"Three hundred dollars. That's a vast amount of money. What do you want it for?"*

---

**THE TRUTH:** (well, mostly the truth. Now her lies are only the lies of omission.)

---

*"To pay taxes on Tara."*

*"So you want to borrow some money. Well, since you're so businesslike, I'll be businesslike too. What collateral will you give me?"*

*"What what?"*

*"Collateral. Security on my investment. Of course, I don't want to lose all that money." His voice was deceptively smooth, almost silky, but she did not notice.*

*Maybe everything would turn out nicely after all.*

---

**VICTORY** – Rhett might loan her the money – but now we can see that Rhett has turned the tables and is playing Scarlett at her own game.

---

*"My earrings."*

*"I'm not interested in earrings."*

*"I'll give you a mortgage on Tara."*

*"Now just what would I do with a farm?"*

*"Well, you could—you could—it's a good plantation. And you wouldn't lose. I'd pay you back out of next year's cotton."*

*"I'm not so sure." He tilted back in his chair and stuck his hands in his pockets. "Cotton prices are dropping. Times are so hard and money's so tight."*

*"Oh, Rhett, you are teasing me! You know you have millions!"*

---

**ROADBLOCK:** Scarlett can feel her chances slipping away. There is more too–ing and fro–ing, and then Scarlett starts to break down and confess the real truth, which takes a monumental effort.

---

*"Rhett, don't! I'll tell you everything. I do need the money so badly. I—I lied about everything being all right. **Everything's as wrong as it could be.** Father is—is—he's not himself. He's been queer ever since Mother died and he can't help me any. He's just like a child. And we haven't a single field hand to work the cotton and there's so many to feed, thirteen of us. And the taxes— they are so high. Rhett, I'll tell you everything. For over a year we've been just this side of starvation. Oh, you don't know! You can't know! We've never had enough to eat and it's terrible to wake up hungry and go to sleep hungry. And we haven't any warm clothes and the children are always cold and sick and—"*

*"Where did you get the pretty dress?"*

*"It's made out of Mother's curtains," **she answered, too desperate to lie about this shame.** "I could stand being hungry and cold but now—now the Carpetbaggers have raised our taxes. And the money's got to be paid right away. And I haven't any money except one five-dollar gold piece. I've got to have money for the taxes! Don't you see? If I don't pay them, I'll—we'll lose Tara and we just can't lose it! I can't let it go!"*

---

Now that Scarlett has told the full truth, Rhett has the upper hand in this power struggle and he presses home his advantage.

---

*"I don't like your collateral. I'm no planter. What else have you to offer?"*

*Well, she had come to it at last. Now for it! She drew a deep breath and met his eyes squarely, all coquetry and airs* *gone as **her spirit rushed out to grapple that which she feared most**. "I—I have myself."*

---

NOTE: In the film, she never said this. He asked what else she had and she looks at him as an *understanding* passes between them. Rhett:

---

*"Just a minute. What makes you think I still want you? What makes you think you are worth three hundred dollars? Most women don't come that high."*
   ***She blushed to her hair line and her humiliation was complete.***
   *"Why are you doing this? Why not let the farm go and live at Miss Pittypat's. You own half that house."*
   *"Name of God!" she cried. "Are you a fool? I can't let Tara go. It's home. I won't let it go. Not while I've got breath left in me!"*

---

This is the absolute truth

---

*"Now, let me get this straight, Scarlett. You are coming to me with a business proposition. I'll give you three hundred dollars and you'll become my mistress."*
   *"Yes." Now that the repulsive word had been said, she felt somehow easier and hope awoke in her again. He had said "I'll give you." There was a diabolic gleam in his eyes as if something amused him greatly.*

---

Rhett has given Scarlett hope – and that's brilliant because it's the hope that kills. (I keep saying that, because it's true!) I love the next few lines, because they absolutely crush Scarlett's hopes.

---

*She was breathing easier now. Being what he was, Rhett would naturally want to torment and insult her as much as possible to pay her back for past slights and for her recent attempted trickery. Well, she could stand it. She could stand anything. Tara was worth it all. "Are you going to give me the money?"*

*He looked as if he were enjoying himself and when he spoke there was suave brutality in his voice.* **"No, I'm not," he said.**

---

(Emotionally, Scarlett hits the wall)

---

*For a moment her mind could not adjust itself to his words.*

*"I couldn't give it to you, even if I wanted to. I haven't a cent on me. Not a dollar in Atlanta. I have some money, yes, but not here. And I'm not saying where it is or how much. But if I tried to draw a draft on it, the Yankees would be on me like a duck on a June bug and then neither of us would get it. What do you think of that?"*

---

GOAL NOW SO COMPLETELY OUT OF REACH, SCARLETT THROWS A TANTRUM.

---

*Her face went an ugly green, freckles suddenly standing out across her nose and her contorted mouth was like Gerald's in a*

EDIT YOUR OWN ROMANCE NOVEL

*killing rage. She sprang to her feet with an incoherent cry which made the hum of voices in the next room cease suddenly. Swift as a panther, Rhett was beside her, his heavy hand across her mouth, his arm tight about her waist. She struggled against him madly, trying to bite his hand, to kick his legs, to scream her rage, despair, hate, her agony of broken pride.*

---

Scarlett has indeed hit rock bottom, (the agony of broken pride, God I love that line) she has no hope at all of paying the taxes on Tara. She's going to lose Tara and she's debased herself in front of Rhett.

---

*"Cheer up," he said, as she tied the bonnet strings. "You can come to my hanging and it will make you feel lots better. It'll even up all your old scores with me—even this one. And I'll mention you in my will."*

*"Thank you, but they may not hang you till it's too late to pay the taxes," she said with a sudden malice that matched his own, and she meant it.*

---

To summarise the entire scene – which is a huge chapter – Scarlett begins with scheming lies and confidence, then ends up telling the truth and in complete despair.

Rhett begins the scene delighted and genuinely happy to see her; he's being truthful. For a moment, he was so taken in he nearly exposed his heart to her. He then lies (by omission, making her think he has the money) then finishes the scene sarcastic and disappointed.

We also saw personal agendas in play. Scarlett wanted Rhett's money. Rhett wanted Scarlett to admit the truth. Rhett won, Scarlett lost.

At the end of this scene, Scarlett is more angry and desperate than she has ever been – and the ticking clock of needing $300 to save her family home is destroying her.

It's utterly fabulous.

# FINDING YOUR TURNING POINTS

*I*t's all very well to take existing movies and novels and show where the turning points are in those. They've already been written.

How do you do it for your own novel?

Pick a scene from your novel – your favourite scene or a random one.

Look at the scene and answer as many of these questions as you can:

- What is happening?
- What needs to happen by the end of the scene?
- How do they get there?
- What is she feeling at the beginning of the scene?
- Depending on the scene: What 'fake' emotion is she projecting to the world to hide how she's really feeling?
- What is he feeling at the beginning of the scene?
- What fake emotion is he projecting to the world to hide how he is really feeling?

- What does she want?
- What does he want?
- Why can't she have what she wants?
- Why can't he as well?
- What is she desperate to keep hidden from him?
- What is she desperate to keep hidden from her?
- What 'secret' information does she know about him that she might bring up?
- Ditto for him?
- What 'emotion leak' do they give away – ie, was there any moment where her emotional mask slips (or his)?
- Does she get what she wants in the scene?
- Does he?
- How is she feeling by the end of the scene?
- What emotions is she trying to keep hidden at this point?
- Same for him – what's he feeling at the end of the scene and what emotions is he trying to keep hidden from her?

This is an exhaustive list. Relax, your scene doesn't need to have every one of these items in it. However, if it's an incredibly pivotal scene, the more turning points – the more of these questions you can answer – the better.

You may not have an answer for every one of these questions, but when you start asking pointed (and sometimes painful) questions of your characters, you find out more about them – and you can really expose their motivations. They will lie to you at first (characters always lie) but after a while you'll get the truth out of them.

Jot your answers down, and keep them front of mind as you edit that scene and put the emotional turning points onto the page.

Not every scene in your novel is going to be as dramatic, emotional and powerful as the 'Scarlett visits Rhett in jail' scene. In fact, an entire book like that would be exhausting. *Gone With The Wind* is exhausting to read, because so many scenes are like this. Scarlett is front and centre, scheming away, constantly second guessing people and desperately trying to get her own way. She never gets a moment's rest, and neither does the reader! She's also far from likeable, but she is compelling because she is engaged in an incredible struggle.

By all means, give yourself permission to have some 'rest' scenes in your novel, so the reader can catch her breath as well. But make sure your major scenes are powered up with these turning points, so you can really pack a punch where it counts.

## PHEW! THAT WAS A LOT OF WORK. CONGRATULATIONS, YOU GOT THERE!

Give yourself a pat on the back!

One you've processed The Staircase of Turning Points through your manuscript, I strongly advise letting it sit again for month or so. If you're in a writers' group, you and another writer friend may want to swap novels and become 'beta readers' together. This is always a great way to get and give advice, as you'll be reading something with fresh eyes, and so will they.

Make sure it's a reciprocal arrangement though – don't approach another writer completely out of the blue and ask them to read your stuff. That's just putting everyone in an awkward situation. So much awkward.

**Where to from here?**

If you're not already a member, join the Romance Writers of Australia (or the equivalent in your country). RWA is an incredible organisation and the members will help you on your road to publication.

Enter competitions – judges often provide great feedback and you'll learn so much.

Attend workshops and check out writing conferences, because they are amazing.

Keep reading your favourite books by your favourite authors.

Above all else, keep writing.

# PART IV

GETTING YOUR BOOKS OUT THERE, IN
FRONT OF READERS

# GET YOUR BOOK INTO AUSTRALIAN LIBRARIES

EBONY MCKENNA

# FOR AUSTRALIAN AUTHORS . . .

## SELL MORE BOOKS, EARN MORE ROYALTIES

This is a special focus on Australian authors. (I'm planning more territory-specific editions in the future, so stay tuned!)

Now that you've edited your brilliant book, you'll be looking for a publisher - or you'll be looking to self publish.

Either way, you'll want to get the book out there, in front of readers. And it would be really nice to make some money.

*Get Your Book Into Australian Libraries* is essential for any Australian author who wants to do just that - get their books onto library shelves.

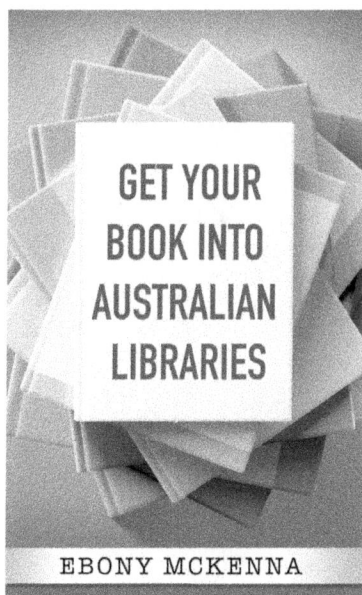

GET YOUR BOOK INTO AUSTRALIAN LIBRARIES

EBONY MCKENNA

I'll take you step-by-step through the process, from buying official ISBNs to registering your titles with official library suppliers.

Then I'll guide you on the best way to contact libraries across Australia (including an exhaustive list of emails) to encourage librarians to order your book from the official suppliers.

Book sales are great, but even better are the Lending Rights that flow afterwards for years to come - royalties Australian creators are entitled to, based on the number of your books on public and school libraries across Australia.

# NOW WHAT?

*There* are so many great writing craft books out there, you really can't go wrong. These are some of my go–to craft books and I do love getting into new ones as well. (Researching is such a great way to put off doing actual writing work.) These books are all very practical and encourage writers to research and write all at the same time.

Kim Hudson, *The Virgin's Promise*
Debra Dixon, *Goal, Motivation, Conflict*
Blake Snyder, *Save The Cat*
James Scott Bell, *Writing Your Novel from the Middle*

Further viewing – because I love movies and I'm so glad these films exist.

Romancing The Stone
Gone With The Wind
Star Wars (Episode IV, A New Hope)
The Princess Bride (because come on, it's The Princess Bride)

When Harry Met Sally

Bridesmaids

Victor /Victoria

Honourable mention: Moulin Rouge, even though it doesn't have a happy ending (well it does, but then the curtain falls and it suddenly doesn't.)

If you've picked up some great writing techniques and ideas from this book, I'd love to hear from you – email me at author@ebonymckenna.com

Please let other writers know what you thought of this book by sharing it with them, and by all means do that 'word of mouth' thing, I hear it really sells books.

Leaving a review on your book buying website of choice is also incredibly welcome.

Thank you very much, you've been awesome.

# ALSO BY EBONY MCKENNA

## THE ONDINE SERIES

Book 1: The Summer of Shambles

Book 2: The Autumn Palace

Book 3: The Winter of Magic

Book4: The Spring Revolution

## OTHER NOVELS

1916–ish

Robyn and the Hoodettes

The Girl & The Ghost

## NON–FICTION

Edit Your Own Romance Novel

Edit Your Own YA Novel

Edit Your Own Science Fiction and Fantasy Novel (coming 2019)

Get Your Book Into Australian Libraries

## ANTHOLOGIES

Dangerous Boys

The Hauntings of Livingstone Hall

# ABOUT THE AUTHOR

Ebony McKenna is the author of seven YA romance novels and several short stories, along with the 'Edit Your Own' series of how-to books.

In 2018, her self-published, self-edited YA novel *The Girl & the Ghost* won the RWA Ruby award for Romantic Book of the Year.

She loves going to AFLW matches to cheer on the Melbourne Demons, and writes match reports for the Women's Footy Almanac.

*Come and waste time with Ebony*
www.ebonymckenna.com
author@ebonymckenna.com

www.ingramcontent.com/pod-product-compliance
Lightning Source LLC
Chambersburg PA
CBHW050726030426
42336CB00012B/1431